Joe & Rose,
Remember our Sligo/Mayo trip
in Sept. '07

Michael

YEATS' LANDSCAPES

FIRST PUBLISHED IN GREAT BRITAIN IN 2000 BY CAXTON EDITIONS
AN IMPRINT OF CAXTON PUBLISHING GROUP
20 BLOOMSBURY STREET LONDON WC1B 3QA

© CAXTON EDITIONS, 2000.

ALL RIGHTS RESERVED. NO PART OF THIS PUBLICATION MAY BE
REPRODUCED, STORED IN A RETRIEVAL SYSTEM OR TRANSMITTED IN ANY
FORM OR BY ANY MEANS, WITHOUT THE PERMISSION OF
THE COPYRIGHT HOLDER.

ISBN 1 84067 142 4

A COPY OF THE CIP DATA IS AVAILABLE FROM THE
BRITISH LIBRARY UPON REQUEST.

ART DIRECTED, DESIGNED AND PRODUCED FOR CAXTON EDITIONS
BY KEITH POINTING DESIGN CONSULTANCY.

REPROGRAPHICS BY GA GRAPHICS
PRINTED AND BOUND IN
SINGAPORE BY STAR STANDARD

ACKNOWLEDGMENTS
MRS AND MRS FENNEY, LISSADELL VIEW, COUNTY SLIGO
EAMON MARTIN, IRENE O'REILLY.

ORIGINAL YEATS WORDS PRINTED BY KIND PERMISSION OF
A.P. WATT LTD AND SIMON AND SCHUSTER ON BEHALF OF
MICHAEL B YEATS

YEATS' LANDSCAPES

TRAVELS WITH WB YEATS

WITH PHOTOGRAPHS BY
VIRGINE AMANT

CAXTON EDITIONS

CONTENTS

INTRODUCTION
7

SLIGO AND LEITRIM
9

DUBLIN
55

GALWAY
89

INTRODUCTION

WB Yeats is often called Ireland's greatest poet and one her finest playwrights. He was born in 1865 of an Anglo-Irish family in Sandymount, a seaside suburb in the South East of Dublin. Childhood was often spent in Sligo where his grandfather was a clergyman to the Church of Ireland in Drumcliff, County Sligo. Many of his most creative years where spent in his home near the home of Lady Gregory in Coole Park, County Galway. In 1922 he was elected to the Senate of the Irish Free State and the following years he was awarded the Nobel Prize for literature. He died in France in 1939 and his body was returned to Ireland in 1948. He is buried in Drumcliff, County Sligo.

SLIGO & LEITRIM

WB Yeats' connection to Sligo goes back to the early 18th century when his grandfather was appointed to the Church of Ireland clergy at Drumcliff in County Sligo. WB Yeats' father married Susan Pollexfen in St John's Church, Sligo. WB Yeats used to visit the area in his school holidays and he returned to Sligo a in adult life, visiting the Gore-Booth sisters in Lissadell House, County Sligo. Many of his poems were inspired by its landscapes.

FISHING BOATS AT MULLAGHMORE, SLIGO

'...memories of Sligo, where I live with my grandparents. I am sitting on the ground looking at a mastless toy boat with paint rubbed and scratched, and I say to my self in great melancholy, 'It is further away than it used to be' and while I am saying it I am looking at a long scratch in the stern, for it is especially the scratch which is further away.'

SLIGO & LEITRIM

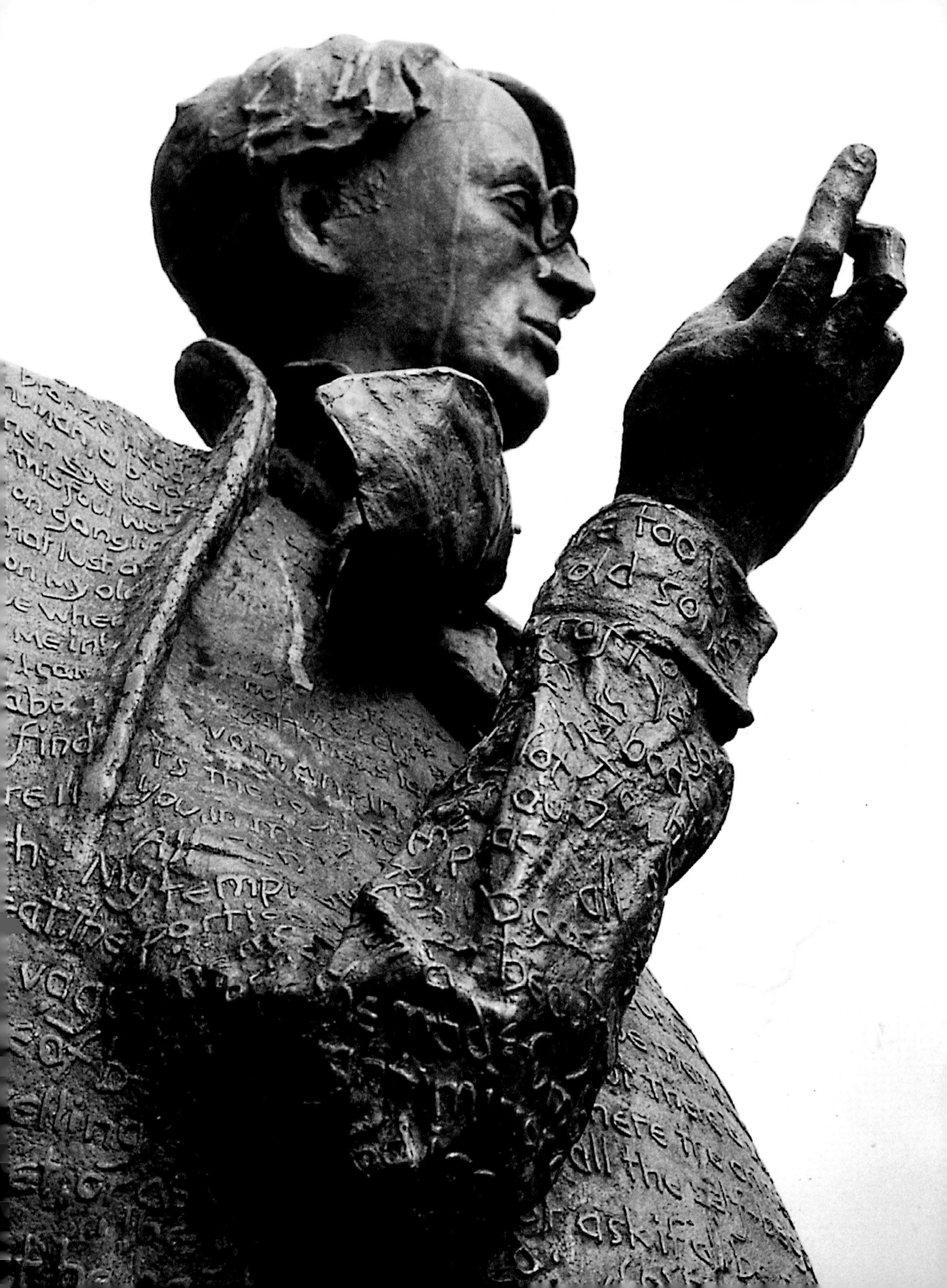

SCULPTURE OF WB YEATS, SLIGO

This modern sculpture is in the centre of Sligo and illustrates the town's close association with the Yeatses. There is a WB Yeats summer school in August and the Niland Collection houses work by WB Yeats' artist brother Jack B. Yeats.

LOUGH GILL

This tranquil lake lies about six kilometres to south of its smaller neighbour Glencar lake. To the right of this picture lies 'The lake Isle of Innisfree'. The poem of the same name is one of Yeats' most famous works.

SLIGO & LEITRIM

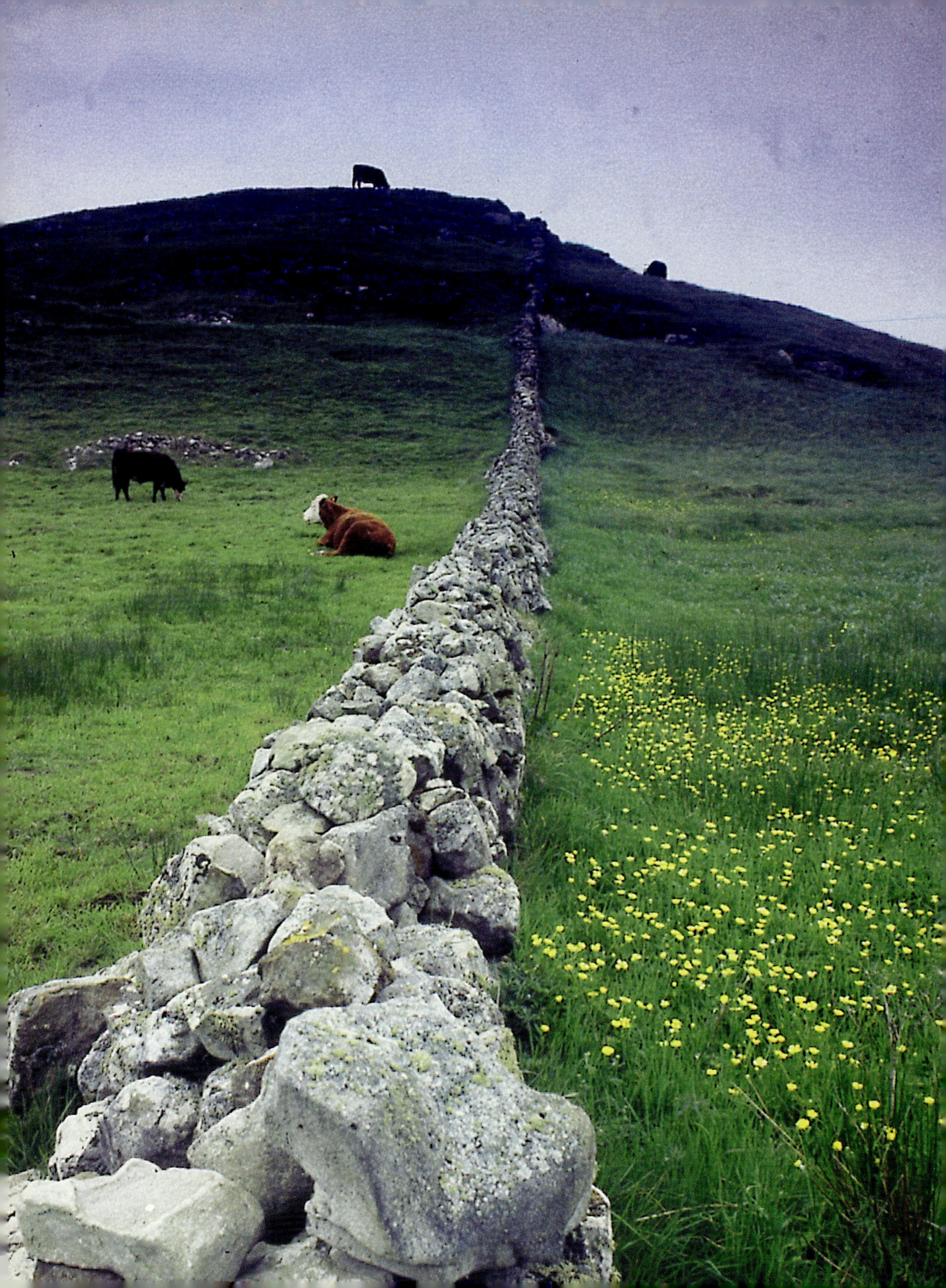

STONE WALLS AT MULLAGHMORE, SLIGO

On the road to Classiebaum Castle, from Mullaghmore fishing village. Mullaghmore is a tiny fishing village with a small harbour and crystal-clear waters.

GLENCAR LAKE

This picturesque lake which lies between the Sligo and Leitrim border, beneath the Dartry Mountains, inspired the poem *The Stolen Child.*

SLIGO & LEITRIM

BEN WISKIN AND BEN BULBEN

Ben Wiskin and Ben Bulben lie beside one another on the edge of the Dartry Mountains. In these mountains lie the Creevykeel Court Tomb of around 3000 years BC and one of the finest such examples in Ireland.

SLIGO & LEITRIM

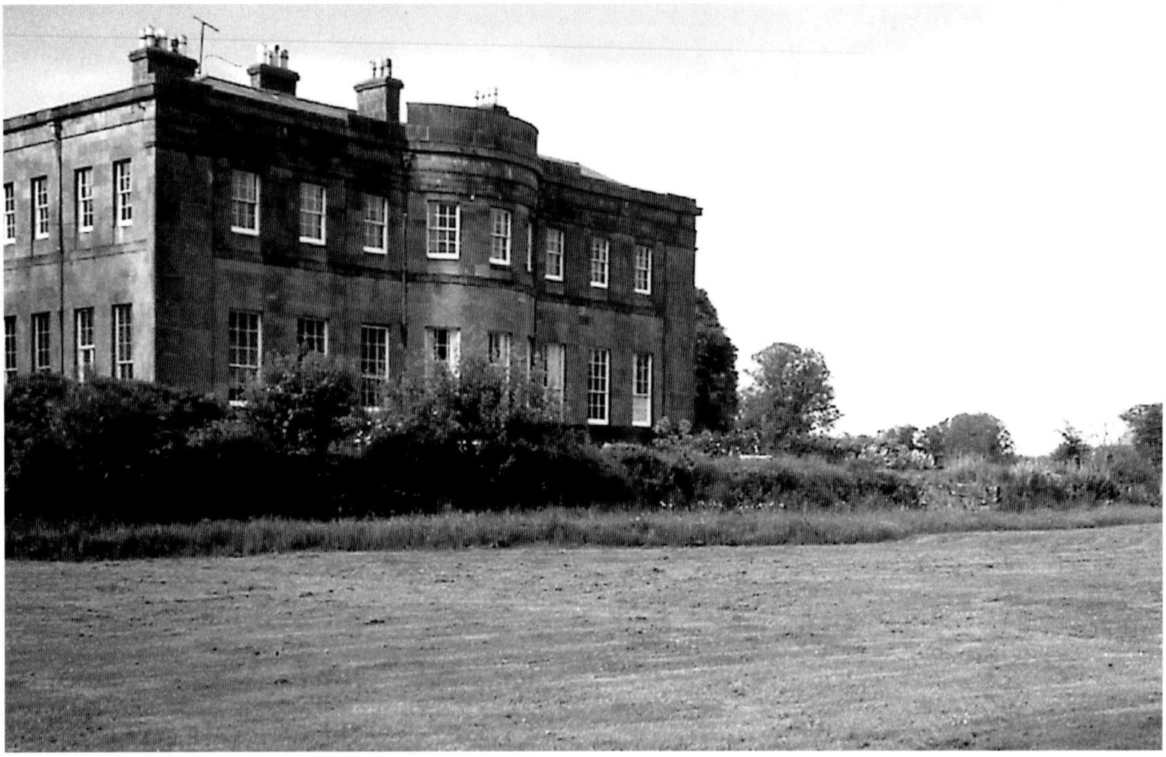

LISSADELL HOUSE, SLIGO

Originally built in the 1830's, this was the home of the Gore-Booth family. Yeats regularly used to visit the sisters, Eva and Constance. They both appeared as 'two girls in kimonos' in his poem *In Memory of Eva Gore-Booth and Con Markiewicz.*

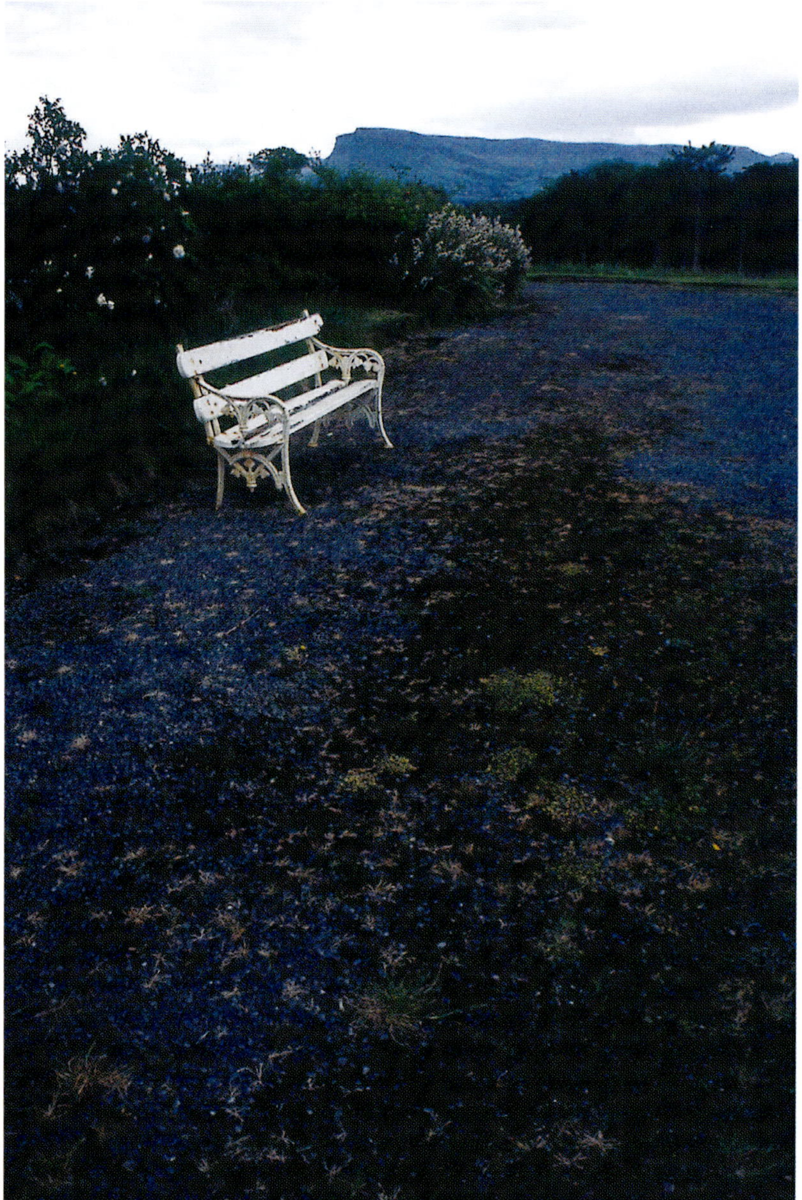

CHAIR AT LISSADELL HOUSE, SLIGO

Yeats used to spend many a leisurely afternoon in Lissadell House. Constance Gore-Booth later married a Polish Count and becoming Countess Markiewicz. She entered politics and became the first woman to be elected to the British House of Commons. Later she became Minister of Labour in the first Irish Government.

VIEW FROM LISSADELL HOUSE

The view from this classical Georgian mansion shows the bay in the distance, where exists a wildfowl reserve.

DUBLIN

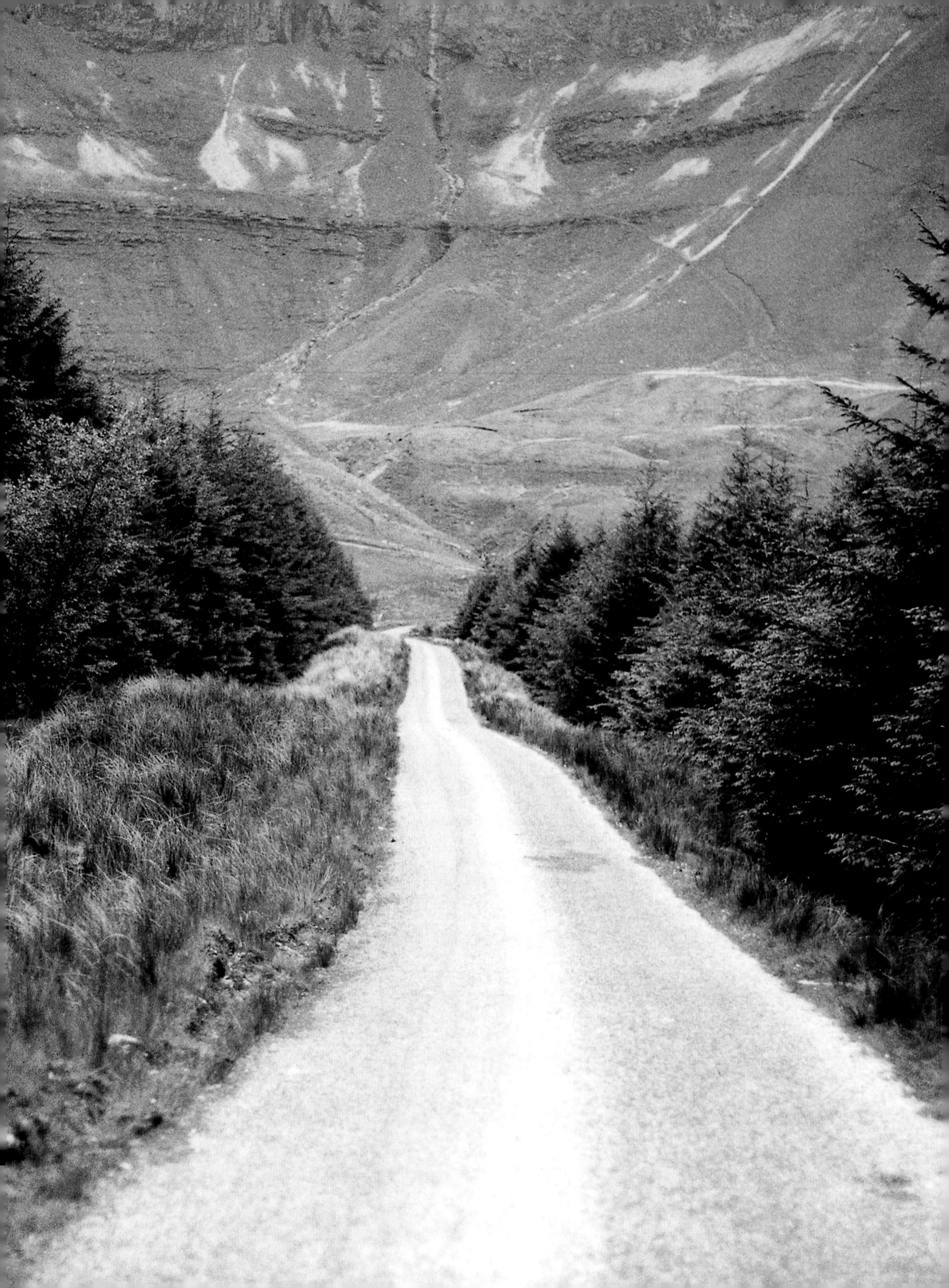

COUNTRY ROAD IN SLIGO AND

LEITRIM BORDERS

The quiet road back from Lough Gill to the centre of Sligo winds across the county border with Leitrim.

VIEWS OF MOTTES

NEAR INNISFREE, LOUGH GILL.

This view, shows in the middle distance, a series of Mottes, which were earthen moulds with flat tops and originally accommodated wooden towers. These were built by the Normans when they first came to Ireland in the 12th century. By the 13th century they needed to consolidate their power and more permanent structures were built. Overleaf shows Lough Gill.

S L I G O & L E I T R I M

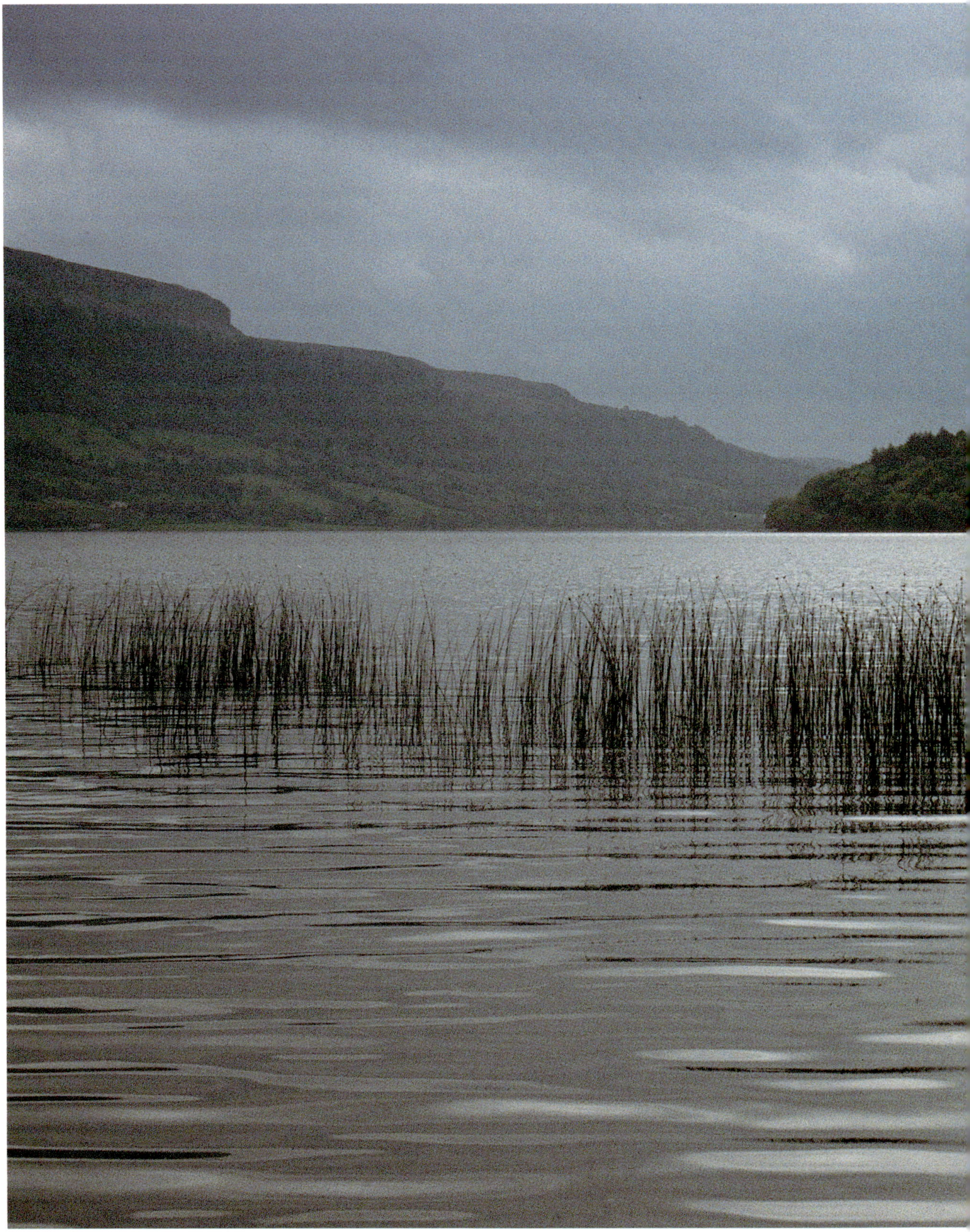

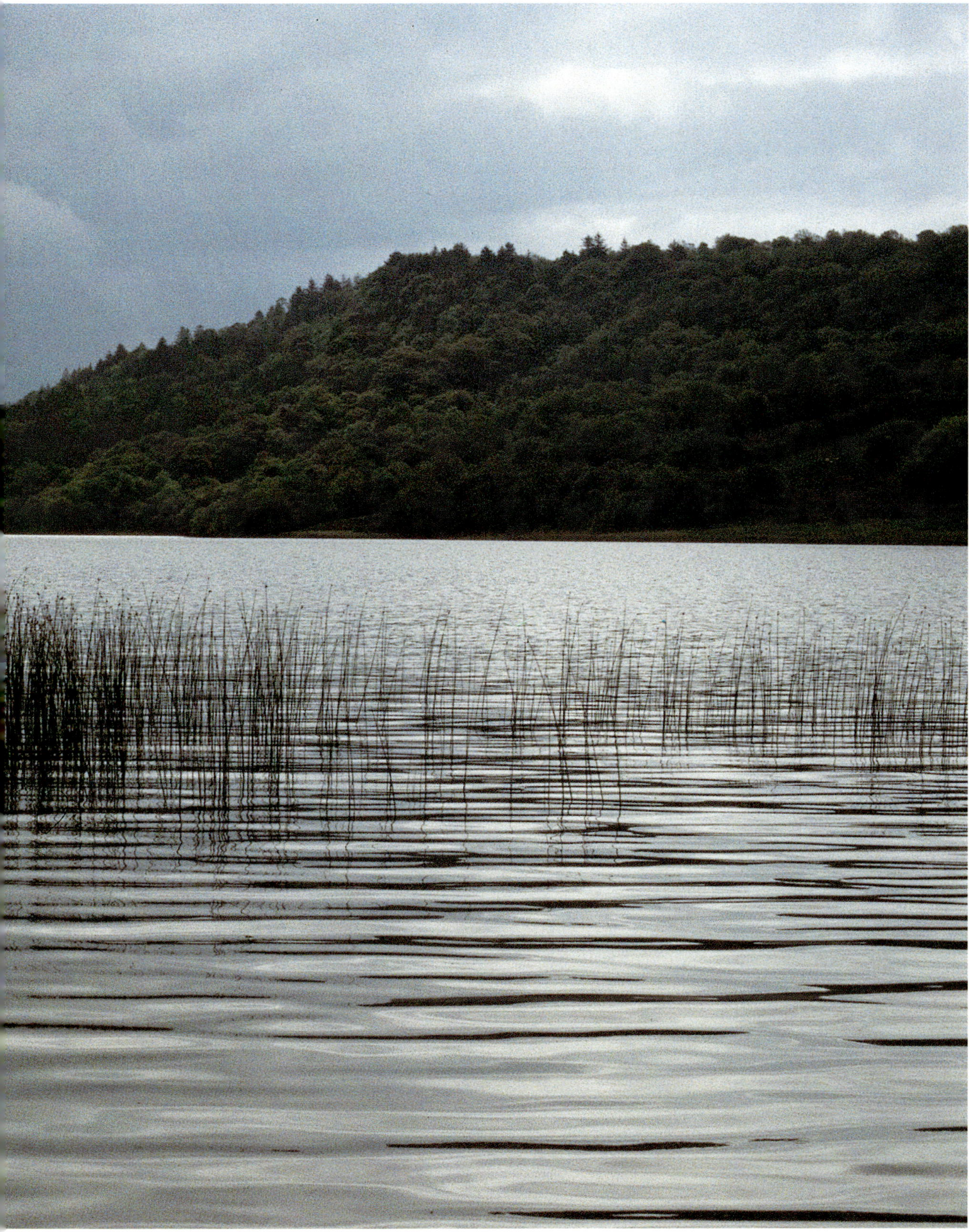

YEATS' LANDSCAPES

BICYCLE LEANING AGAINST
SANDSTONE WALL IN SLIGO.

Sligo was so named after *Sligeach*, meaning the Shelly River. It lies at the mouth of the River Garavogue, and is the largest town in the North West of the Republic of Ireland. Megalithic remains show that there have been settlements in the area since 3000BC.

PARKES CASTLE, LOUGH GILL, LEITRIM

This is a 17th century fortified plantation manor house, which overlooks Lough Gill on the Leitrim and Sligo border. It is so named after the English family which gained possession of it during the 1620 plantation of Leitrim. The castle was originally a stronghold of the O'Rouke clan, rulers of the kingdom of Breffni.

SLIGO & LEITRIM

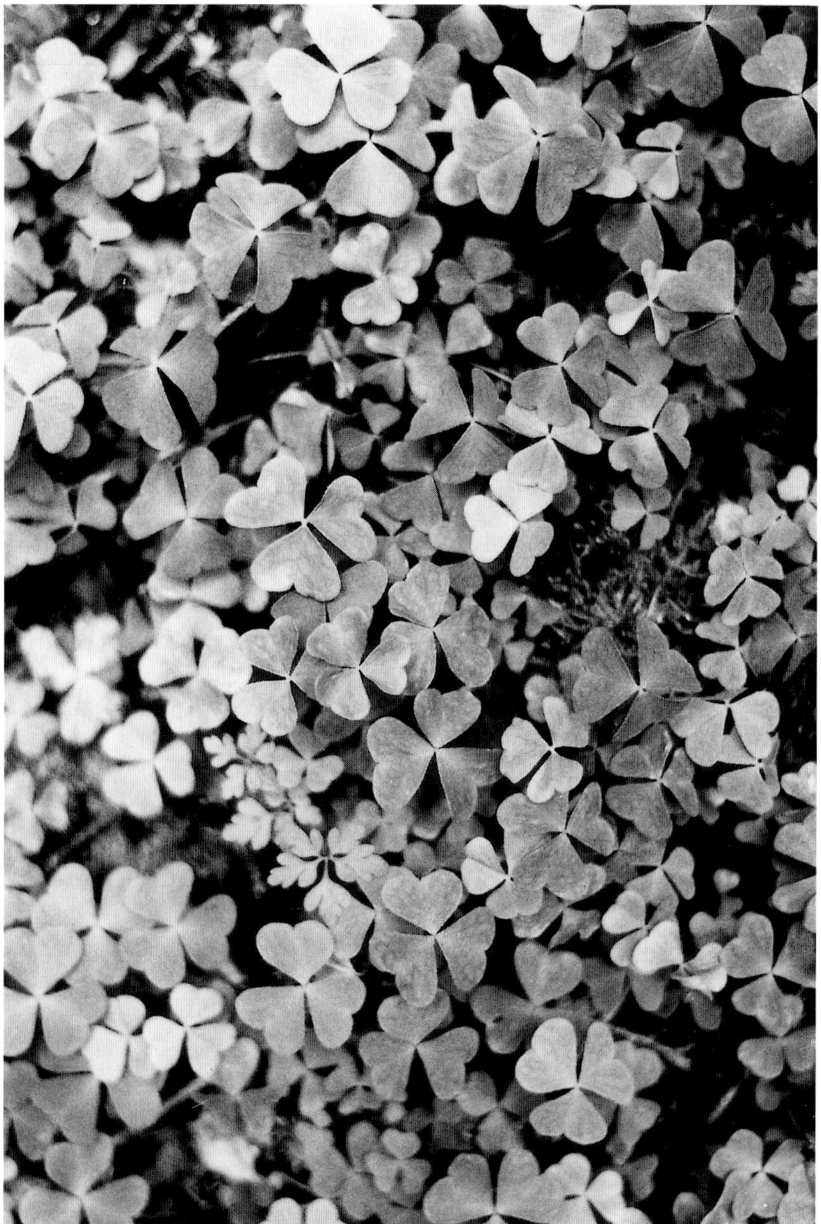

FOREST FLOOR

Overlooking Lough Gill, are beautiful woods, which are said to have inspired many of Yeats love poems such as *Down by the Salley Gardens.*

WATERFALL AT GLENCAR

A short walk from Glencar lake lies the magical waterfall celebrated in his poem *The Stolen Child.* The fall is nearly fifteen meters.

SLIGO & LEITRIM

YEATS' LANDSCAPES

LOUGH GILL

This is the view to the left of Innisfree and subject of one of Yeat's most famous works, *Lake Isle of Innisfree.*

BEN BULBEN FROM ROSSES POINT

Yeats was finally laid to rest in Drumcliffe Church yard in accordance with his wishes to be buried under Ben Bulben.

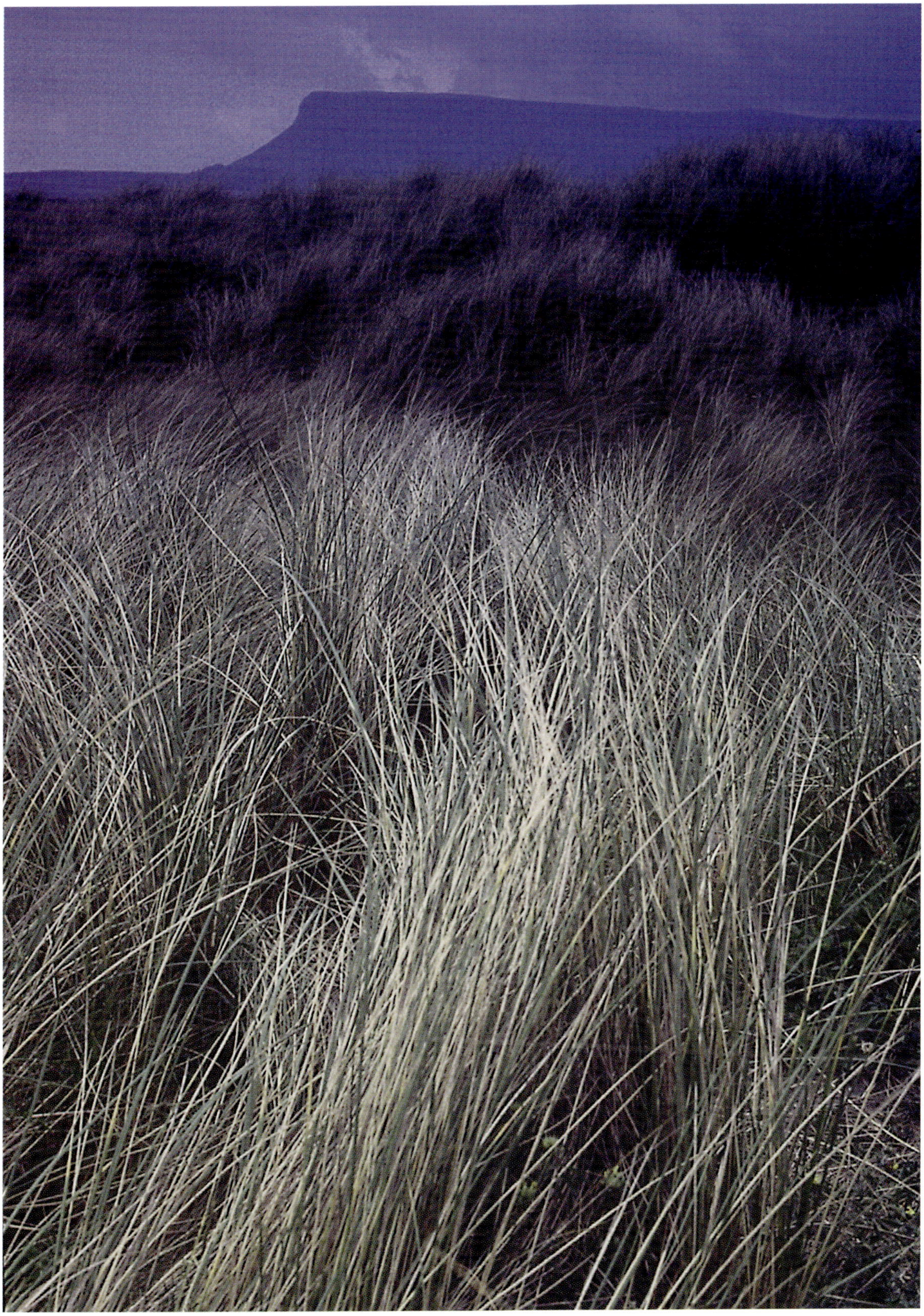

COUNTRY LANE, SLIGO

Farming can still appear today to have a relaxed pace of life of Yeats day. This lane winds up near the mountains of Ben Wiskin and Ben Bulben.

SLIGO & LEITRIM

YEATS' LANDSCAPES

COUNTRY LANDSCAPE, SLIGO

Yeats loved the landscape of Sligo and it was the inspiration of some of his greatest work. He wished to return to Drumcliff church, his final resting place.

ROSSES POINT

Yeats wrote movingly of his how he and his sister would listen for hours to stories told by his mother of pilots and fishing-people from Rosses Point. She also spoke of her own childhood and Yeats said 'it was always assumed between us that Sligo was more beautiful than other places.'

SLIGO & LEITRIM

YEATS' LANDSCAPES

VIEW OF CLASSIEBAWN CASTLE, SLIGO

The castle built in 1874 and overlooking the bay towards Inishmurray Island was first the home of Viscount Palmerston. It was then the home of the Mountbatten family until Lord Mountbatten and three others were murdered by the IRA while on a boat trip in Mullaghmore in 1979. It is now in private hands and not open to the public.

DUBLIN

WB Yeats was born at 'Georgeville' 5, Sandymount Avenue, Dublin. He left Dublin for schooling in Hammersmith, London, always returning to Sligo for holidays. He then returned with his family when 15 years old to Howth, which overlooks the northern entrance to Dublin Bay, travelling each morning to his father's studio near St Stephen's Green in the heart of the city. He later established the Abbey Theatre, in Lower Abbey Street and when he became a Senator he lived in Merrion Square. His last home in Ireland was in the village of Rathfarnham, near Dublin.

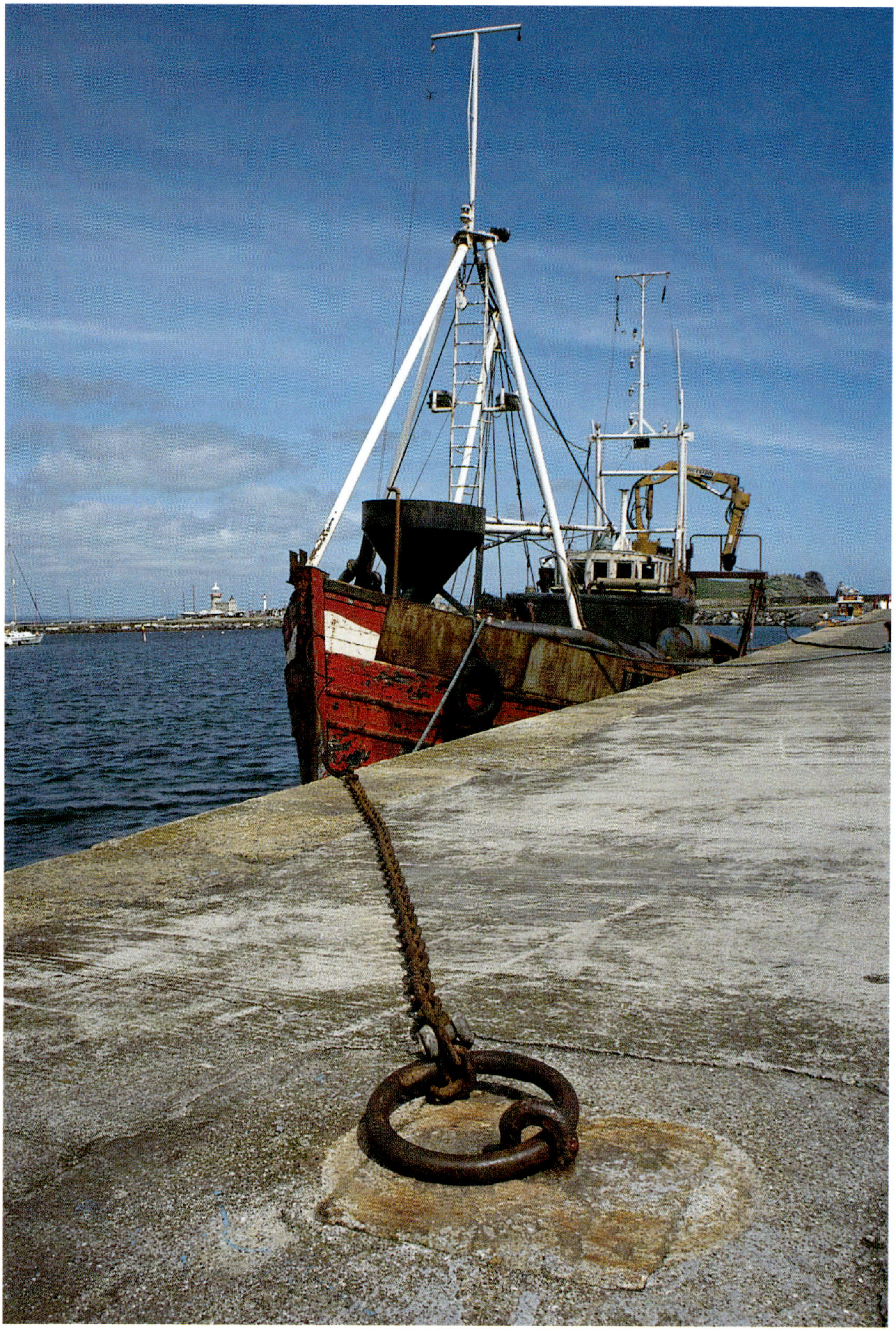

FISHING BOATS AT HOWTH

Yeats spent the last of his childhood in Howth. He left London in 1880, at the age of fifteen, where he had been attending school in Hammersmith, and the family took a thatched cottage on the top of the cliffs overlooking Howth. The Yeates employed a local woman and WB listened to tales of faery-haunted hills and woods.

FISHING BOATS AT HOWTH

Howth still as picturesque as was in Yeats youth and has an active fishing industry being one of Ireland's most important fishing ports.

DUBLIN

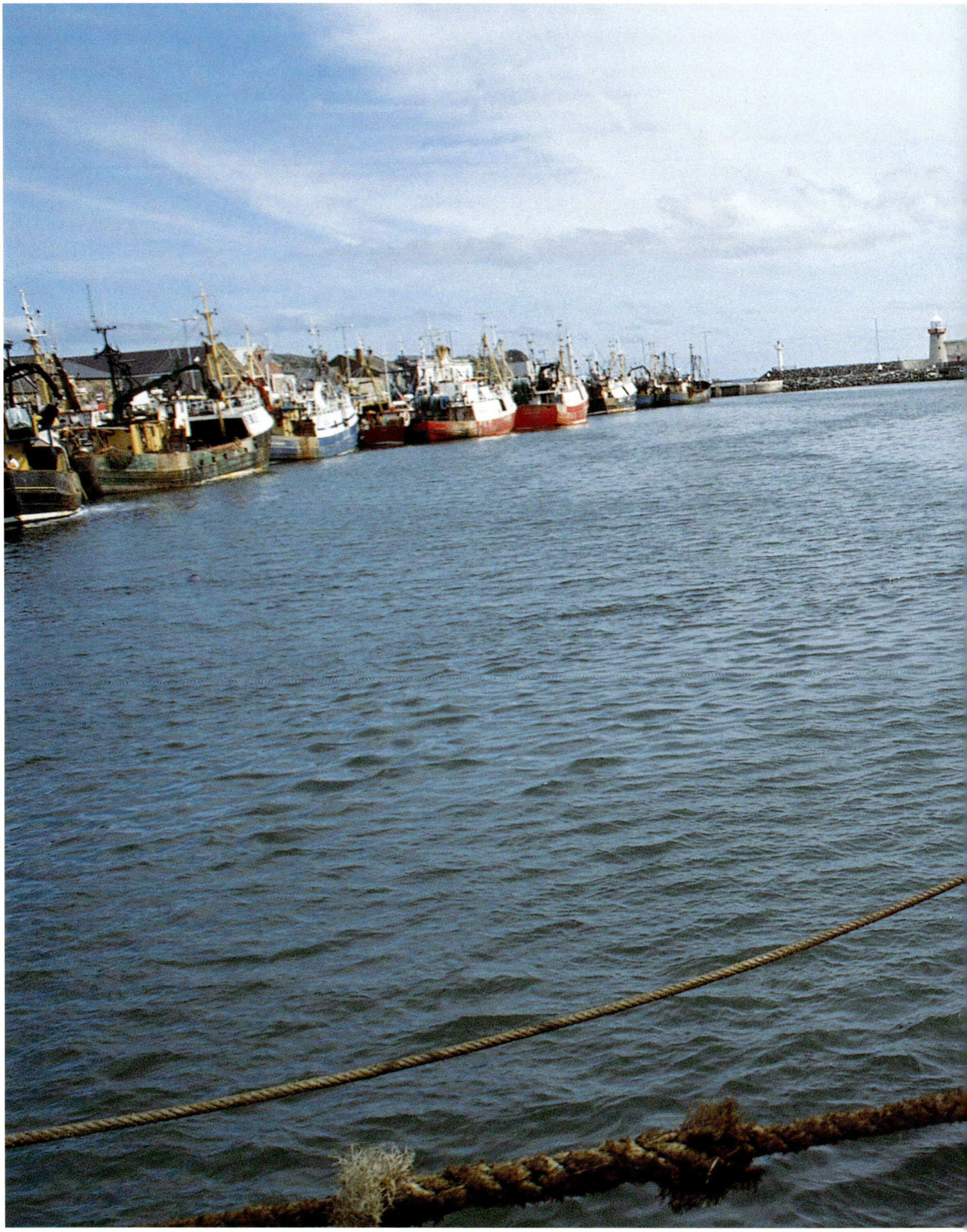

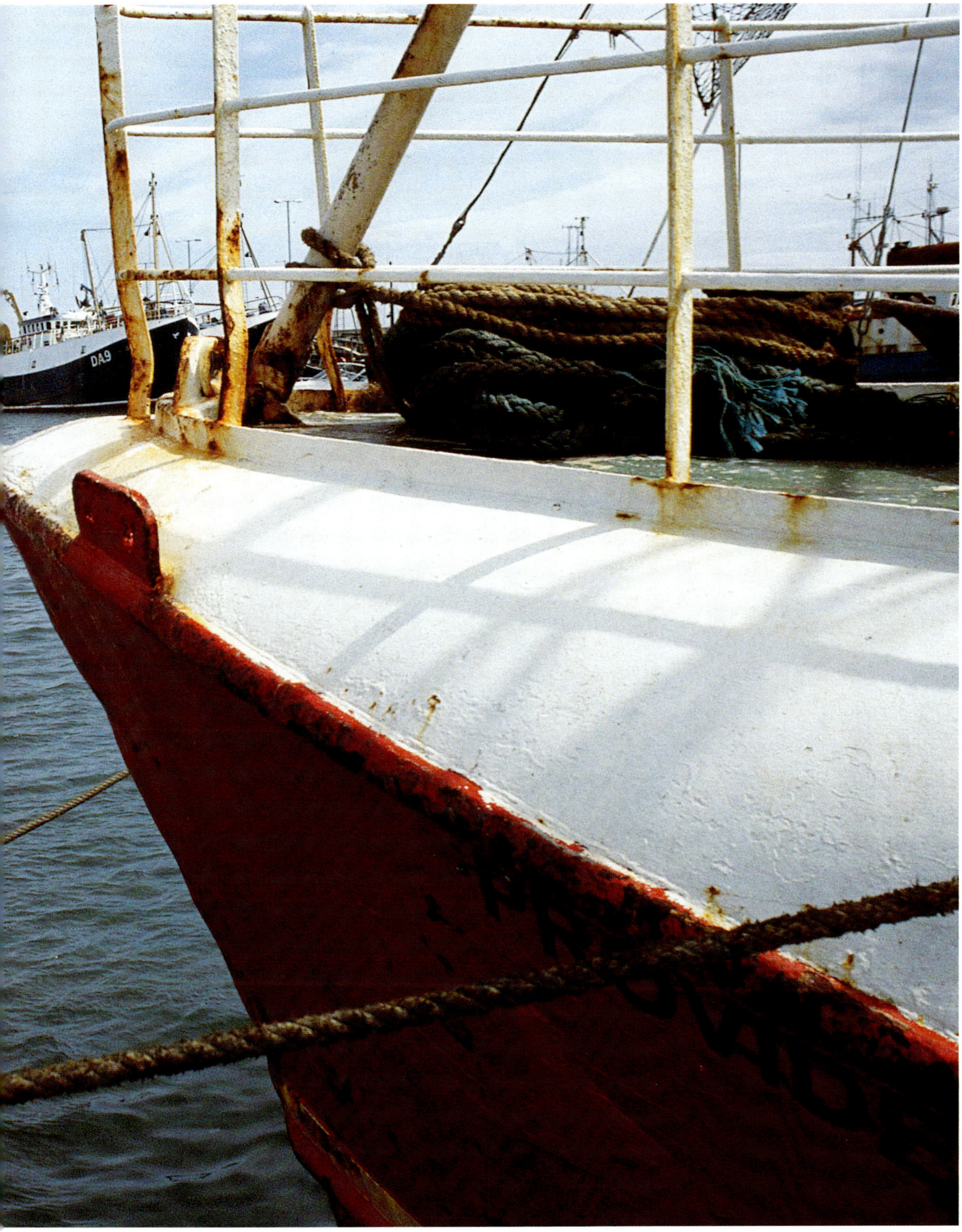
DA9

THE HARBOUR AT HOWTH

Apart from the fishing industry, Howth is now not only a very fashionable place to live but is a major yachting centre.

DUBLIN

YEATS' LANDSCAPES

POST BOX IN DUBLIN

Yeats' father, John, was a painter, and while living in Howth, he would take his son by train to the centre of Dublin and they would eat breakfast in his studio in York Street, close by St Stephen's Green.

CARVED HEAD ON CHAPEL ROYAL
AT DUBLIN CASTLE

The Castle was the centre of British rule for over 700 years. Fittingly, it was here that British administration handed over power to the new Free state of Michael Collins. Yeats became a member of Seanad Éireann, the Irish Senate. He was offered the seat in 1922 which he accepted and took up on January 13th 1923.

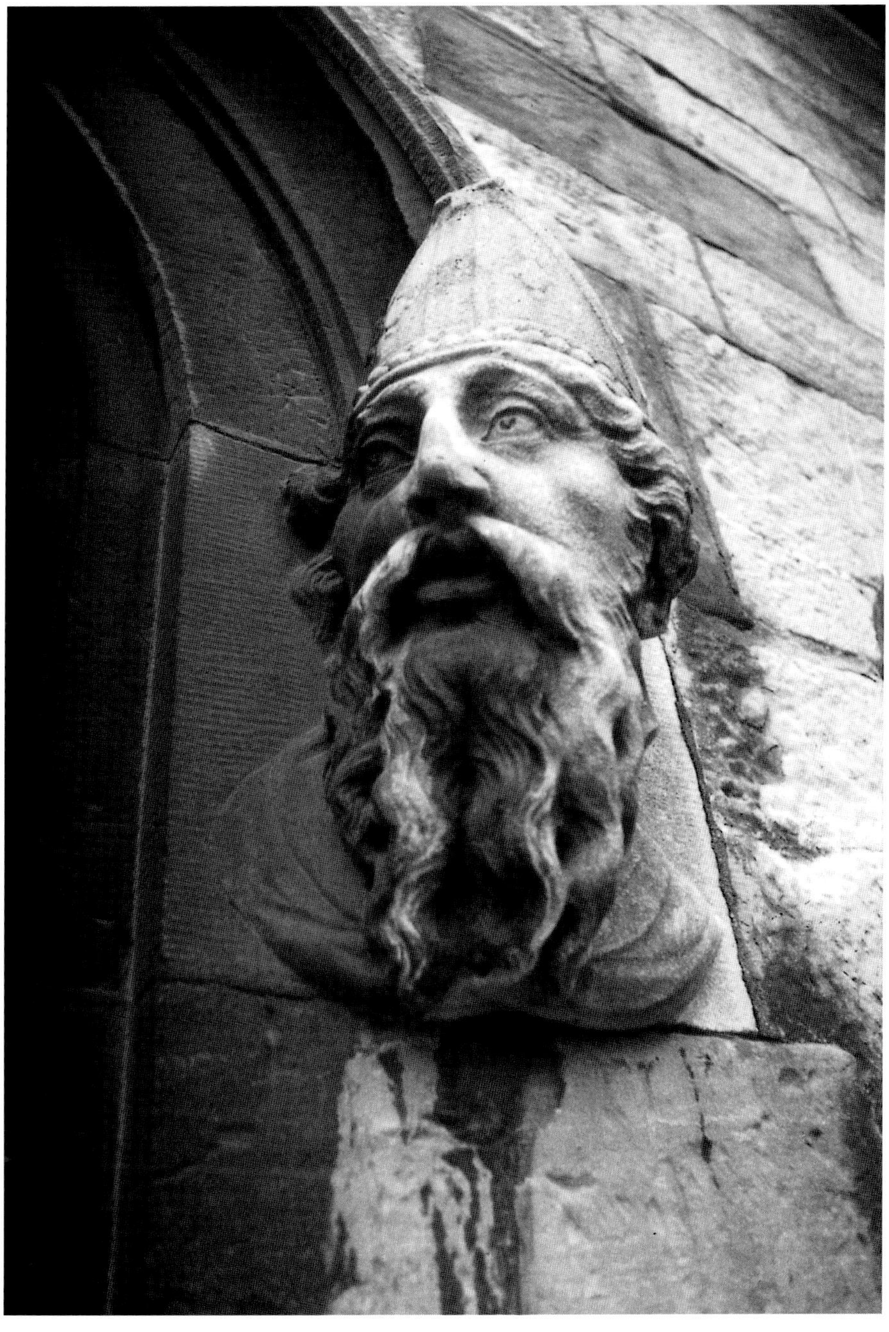

SANDYCOVE

As well as being the birthplace of Yeats, it is also where James Joyce lived in 1904 in the Martello Tower. These towers were built in a series along the coast in the 19th century to deter Napoleonic invasions. The tower now houses a permanent exhibition devoted to Joyce. Sandymount Green commemorates Yeats association with the area by a sculpture of the poet.

DUBLIN

YEATS' LANDSCAPES

TRINITY COLLEGE

Trinity College was founded in 1591 by Elizabeth 1 on the site of an old monastery. Most of the buildings date from the mid eighteenth century. Yeats, unlike his father, grandfather and great grandfather, did not go to the college. His father had wanted him to attend, but Yeats has written 'I did not tell him that neither my classics nor my mathematics were good enough for any examination.'

SCULPTURE IN MERRION SQUARE

Laid out in 1762, this is attractive park, is opposite where Yeats twice lived. He first lived at 52 and then later at 82 when he was a senator of the Irish Free State. Other people who lived along the street included Oscar Wilde when a boy, Daniel O'Connell and Sheridan Le Fanu, author of *Carmilla*.

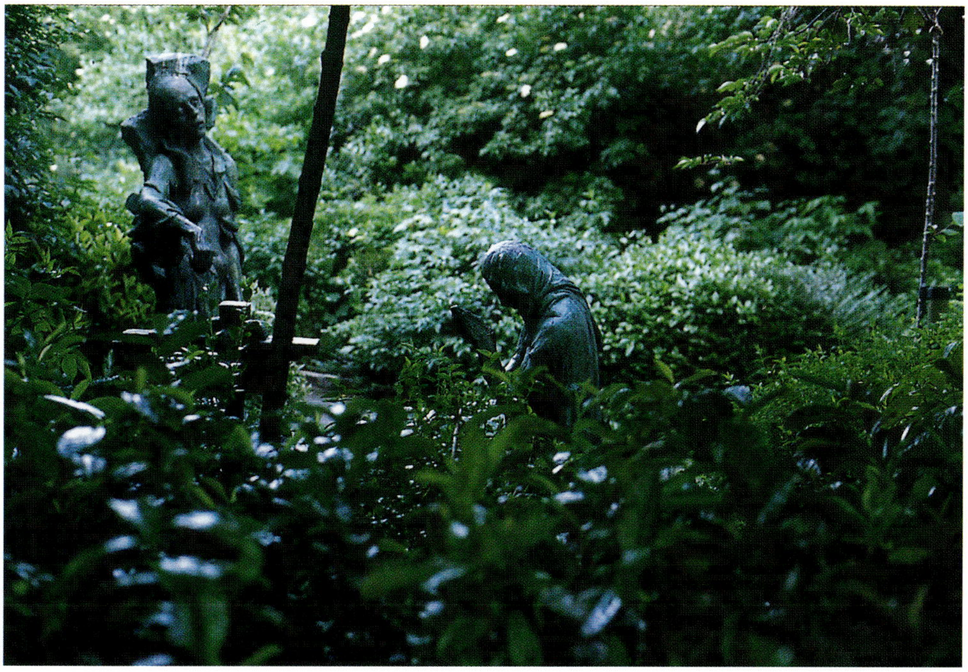

YEATS' LANDSCAPES

THE SACRED HEART OF JESUS
IN O'CONNELL STREET.

O'Connell Street was laid out in the mid-18th century as Sackville Street, and was one of Europe's most elegant promenades. Much of the original street was wrecked during the 1916 Rising and suffered further wreckage in the Civil War of 1922. The Street in Yeats' day was dominated by a tall column topped by Admiral Lord Nelson and was erected in 1815 to mark his famous sea victory over the French in Trafalgar. It pre-dated by 32 years the similar edifice in Trafalgar square and was destroyed by unknown republicans in 1966 to mark the 50th anniversary of the Rising.

YEATS' LANDSCAPES

THE GENERAL POST OFFICE IN O'CONNELL STREET.

The building was seized by the Easter rebels in 1916, during the middle of the first world war, proclaiming it as their headquarters. When they were eventually captured, the initial bemusement of the Dubliners 'changed utterly' said Yeats in his poem *Easter 1916* when 15 of the insurgents were executed. Pock-marks are still visible from bullets fired during the fighting.

THE CUSTOM HOUSE

Architect James Gandon was commissioned by John Beresford, the unpopular first commissioner of the revenue to design the building and it was completed in 1791. It was a major centre for British power until it was gutted by fire in 1921 before the treaty. It was rebuilt in the first years of the new Irish government.

DUBLIN

YEATS' LANDSCAPES

THE FUSILERS ARCH,
ST STEPHEN'S GREEN, DUBLIN

St Stephen's Green is a small informal park bordered by elegant houses. It was formerly a common in 1663 and was not surrounded by houses until the 18th century. The Guinness family in 1880 gave the money to lay out formal gardens as a public park.

THE WRITERS MUSEUM, DUBLIN

This building was opened in 1991 in an 18th century house, which displays memorabilia of Yeats and other leading Irish writers. It is also a venue for readings and seminars.

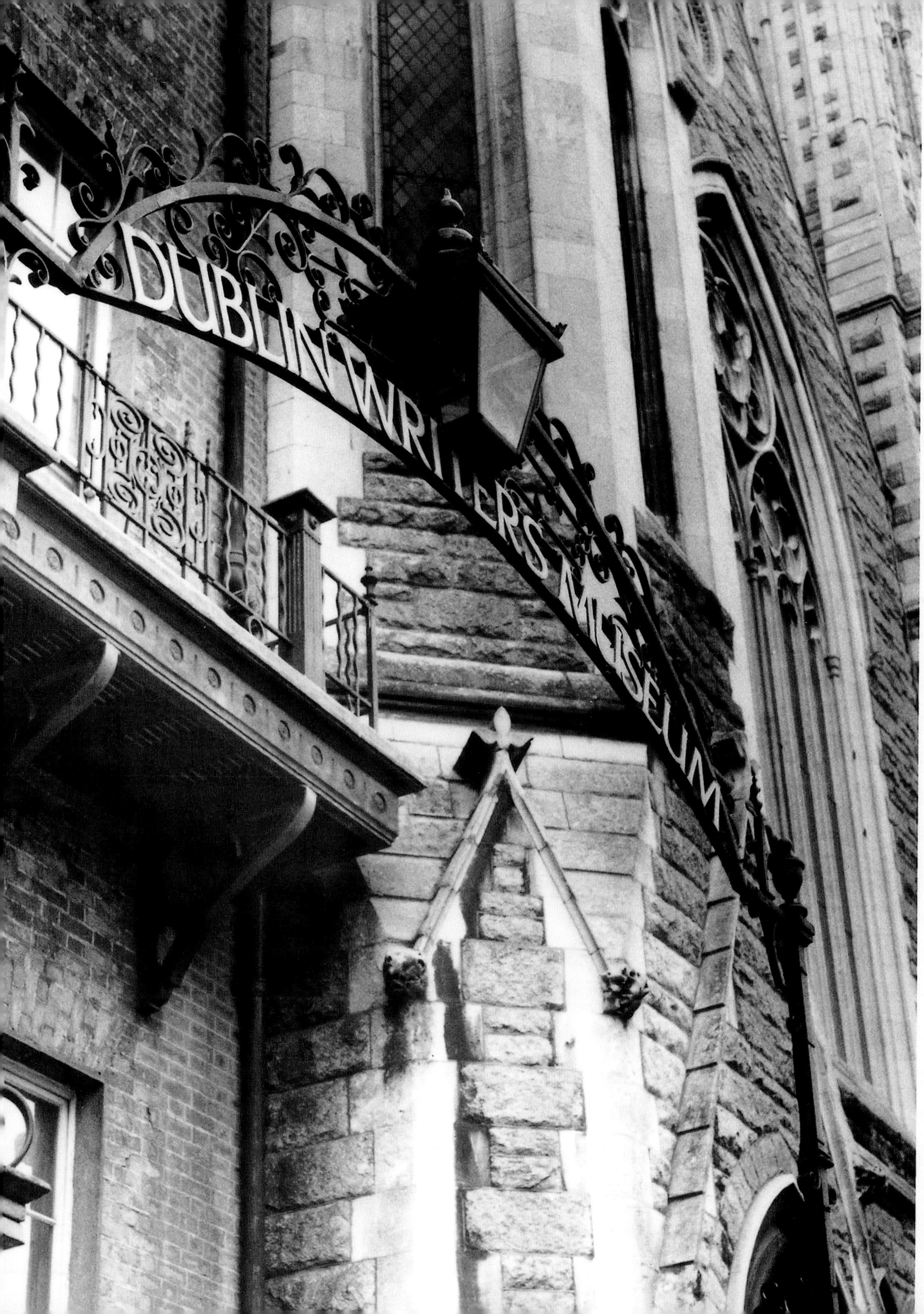
DUBLIN WRITERS MUSEUM

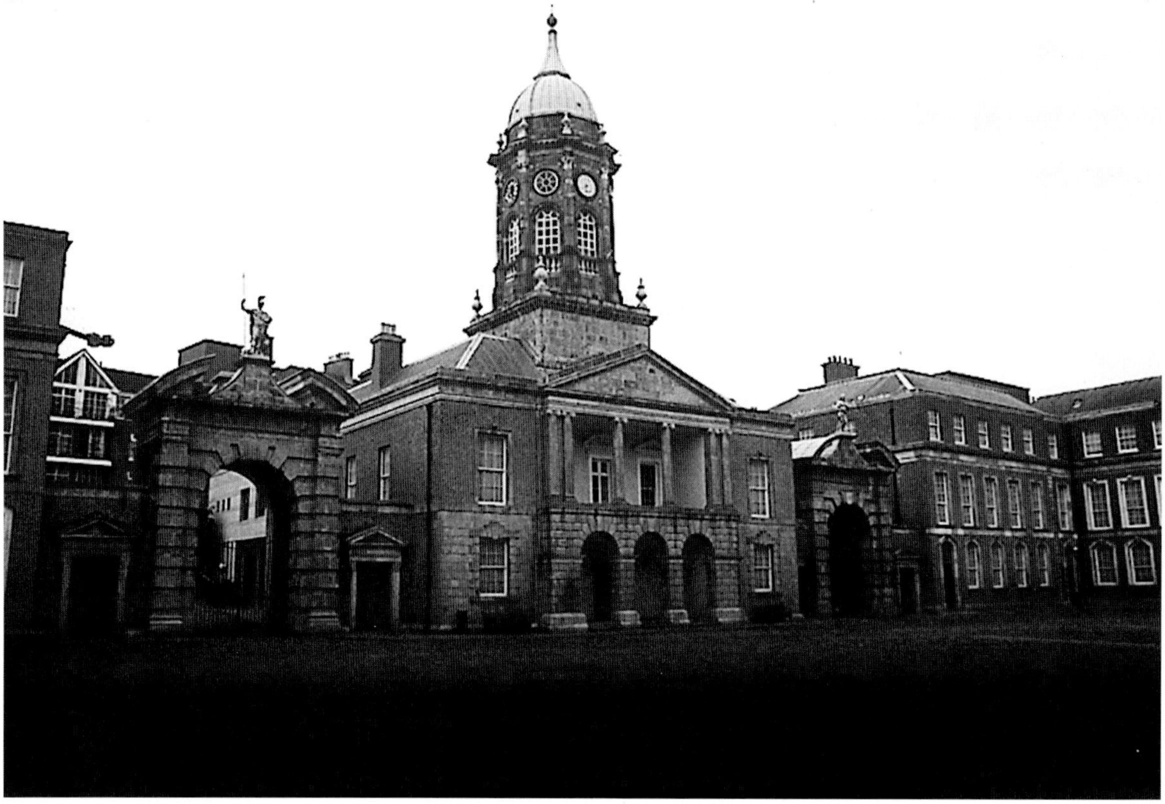

DUBLIN CASTLE

Although dating back to 1202, when it was a Norman castle, it was largely ruined by fire in 1684. The present building mainly dates from the 18th century.

THE NATIONAL GALLERY OF IRELAND, DUBLIN

The sculpture in the front is of the National Gallery of Ireland is of the Irish railway tycoon William Dargan. He organised the 1853 Dublin Exhibition on this site and the profits of which were used to start the gallery's collection.

DUBLIN

GALWAY

Yeats spent much of his later years in the south of Galway where he was often stayed as the guest of Lady Gregory in her house and grounds at Coole Park, just outside Gort. He first met Lady Gregory in 1898 and she entertained many leading literary and artistic figures of the day, including Bernard Shaw, Sean O'Casey, Augustus John and John Masefield. In 1917 Yeats acquired a summer home with his wife George Hyde-Lees at Thoor Ballylee, a nearby tower by the side of a stream and made frequent visits to Coole.

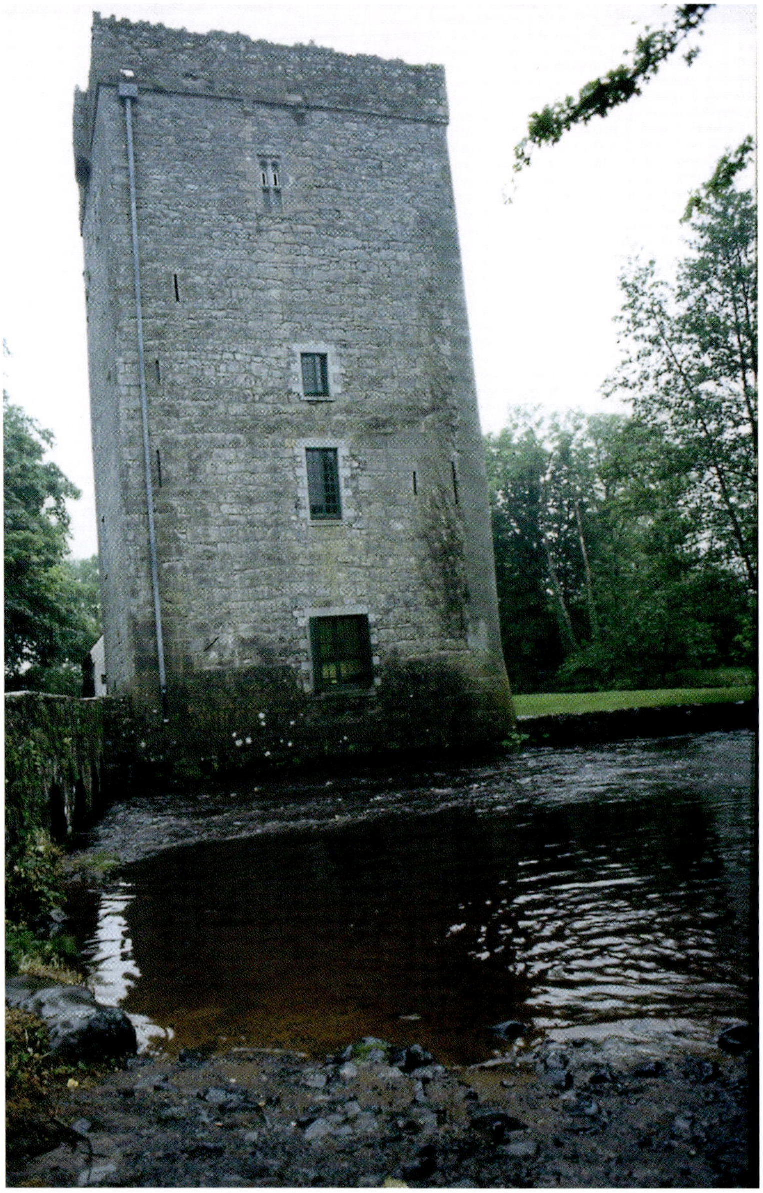

THOOR BALLYLEE

The tower, originally a Norman fortified house, was owned by the de Burgo family in the 13th and 14th centuries. It passed through various ownerships and in 1916 Yeats bought it as his summer house for £35. In 1917, having married Miss George Hyde-Lees, he settled there. It was the setting of *The Winding Stair* and *The Tower* Poems and while here Yeats and Lady Gregory at Coole House helped establish the Abbey Theatre in Dublin.

ENTRANCE TO COOLE PARK

The entrance to the park is through an avenue of ilex trees, which leads to the foundations of the house which is all that remains of the house that was headquarters of the Irish Literary Revival. Yeats spent over thirty summers there and often winters too. It was an orderly house and Lady Gregory provided the peace and inspiration which Yeats never ceased to celebrate.

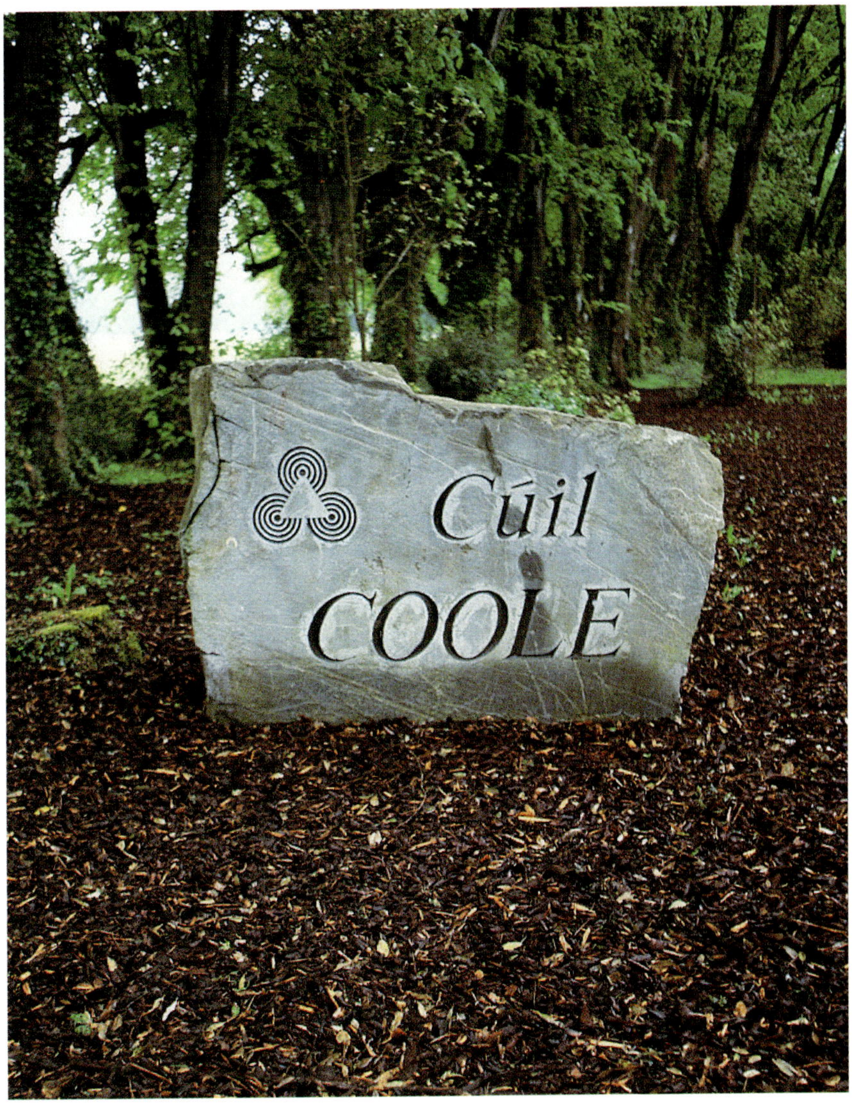
Cúil
COOLE

YEATS' LANDSCAPES

REMAINS AT COOLE PARK

The melancholic prophecy in the final verse of *Coole Park, 1929* anticipated the destruction of the great house. In 1927 Lady Gregory had been forced to sell the house and land to the Forestry Department, but had been allowed to live there until her death in 1932. Thereafter the house was cleared of its contents and the house was eventually demolished in 1941.

REMAINS OF COOLE HOUSE

Coole was demolished in 1941 during the second world war and after the deaths of Lady Gregory and Yeats. Yeats foresaw the houses fate in the last stanza of *Coole Park, 1929*, when he wrote of 'nettles wave upon a shapeless mound'.

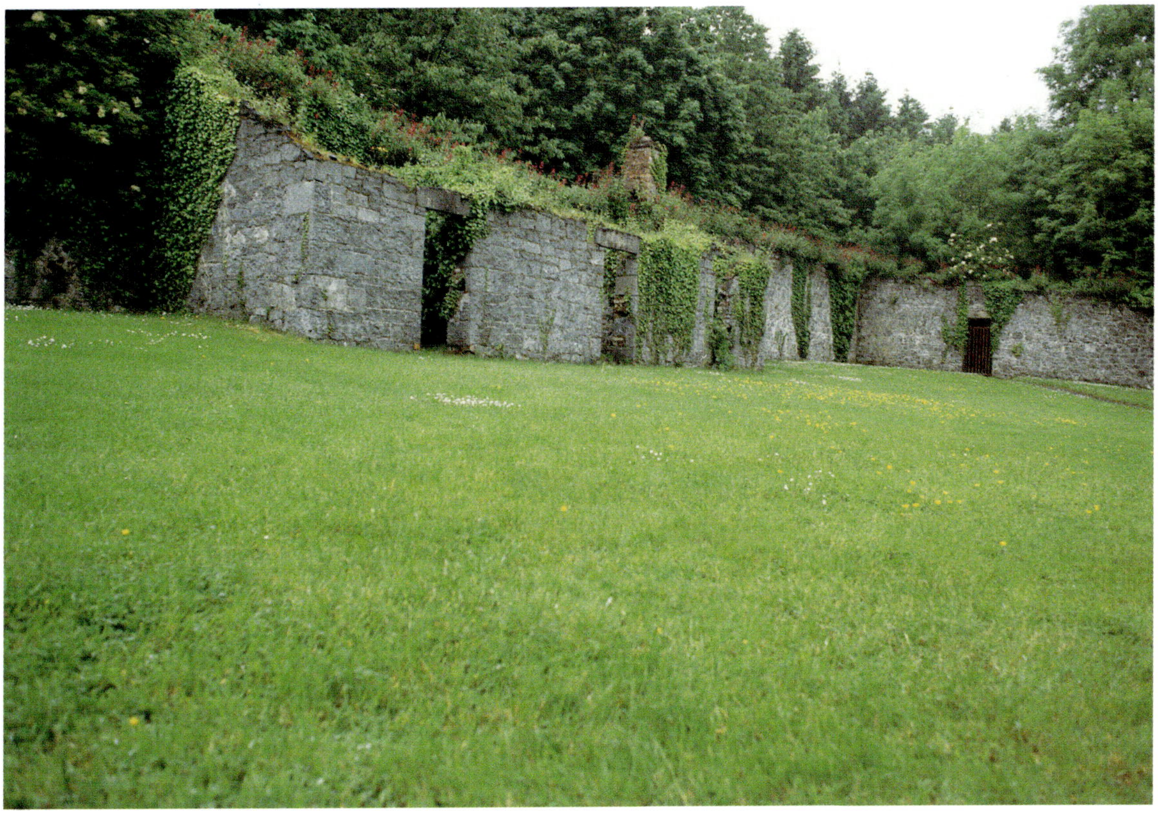

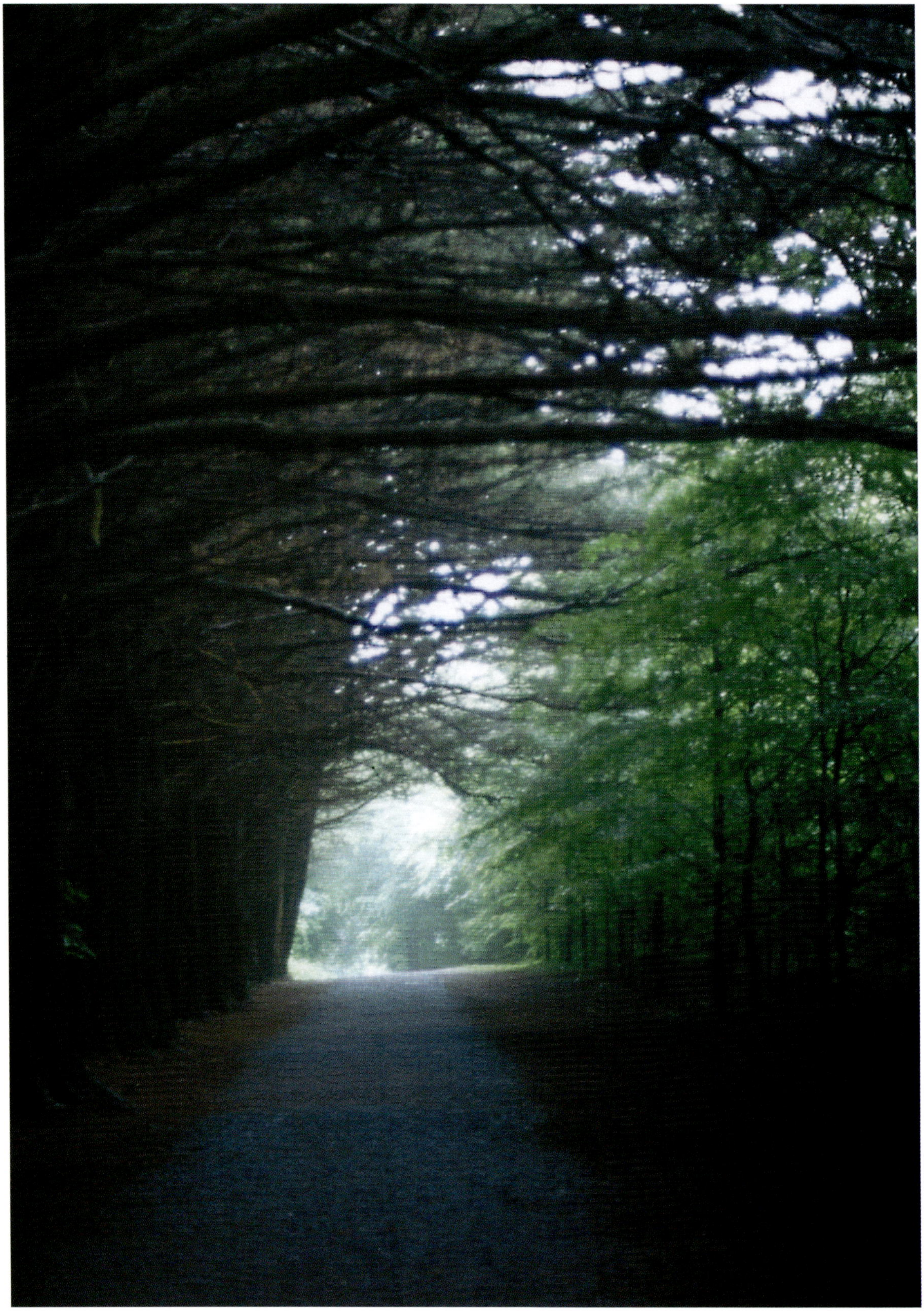

PATH TO COOLE LAKE

The journey that Yeats would frequently make walking to the Lake in Coole Park would take some minutes as he walked down this tree-lined avenue.

COOLE LAKE

Saint Colman, who is supposed have associations with the lake, is held in honour throughout Ireland and to have done many kindnesses. One such story is of a boy who was sent by a farmer to drive the birds from his crops and on one day it was so hot, that was scared that if he fell asleep, he would be beaten by the farmer. So he prayed to Saint Colman who called the birds into a barn where they stopped and the crops remained untouched.

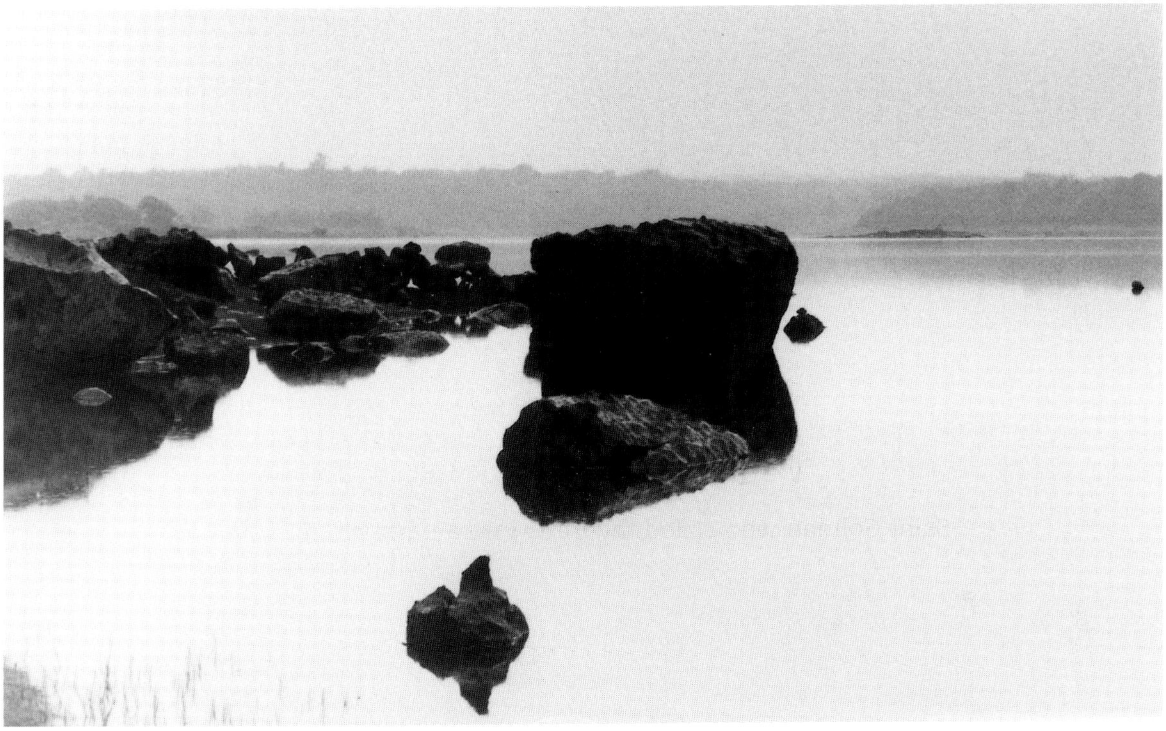

THE GRAVE OF THE POET ANTHONY RAFTERY

The poet (1784-1835) was born at Cill Liadáin Killeden, Kiltimagh, County Mayo. He lived most of his life in South Galway lived near the tower (Thoor Ballylee) and wrote of the local beauty Mary Hynes. He is buried at the cemetery of the poets, Killeeneen, Galway.

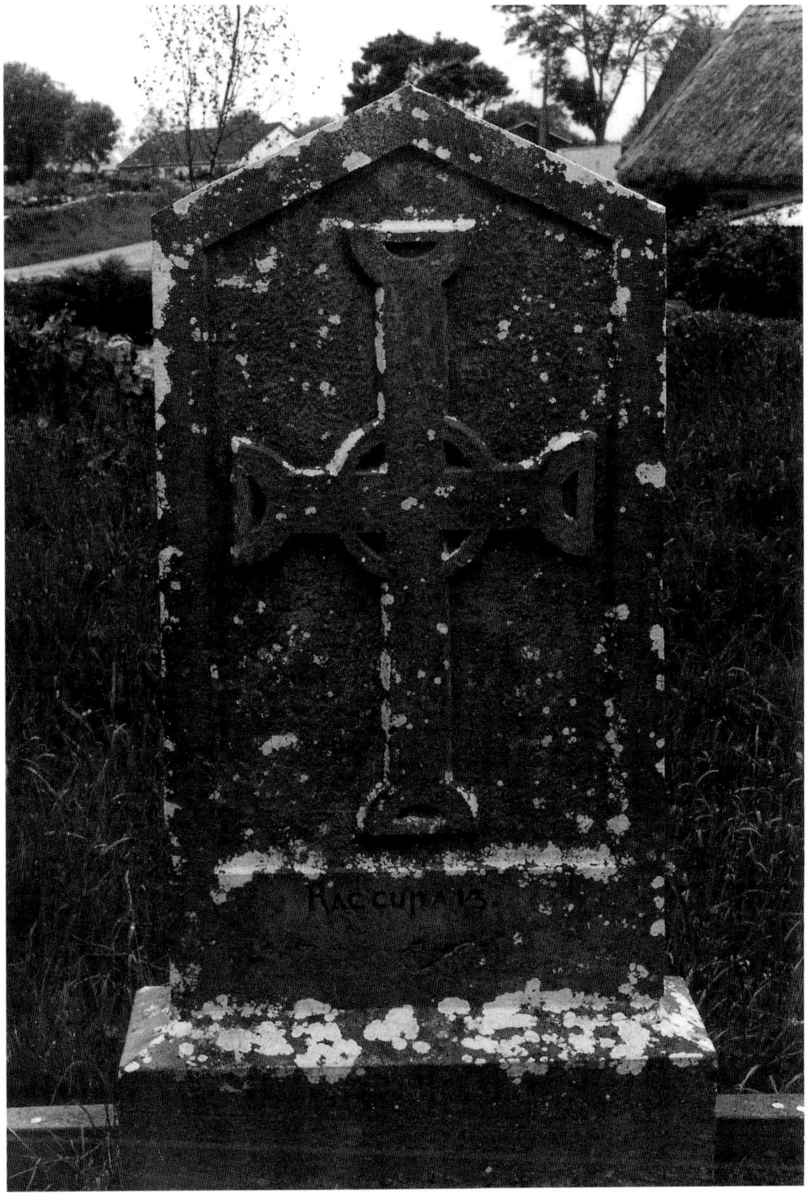

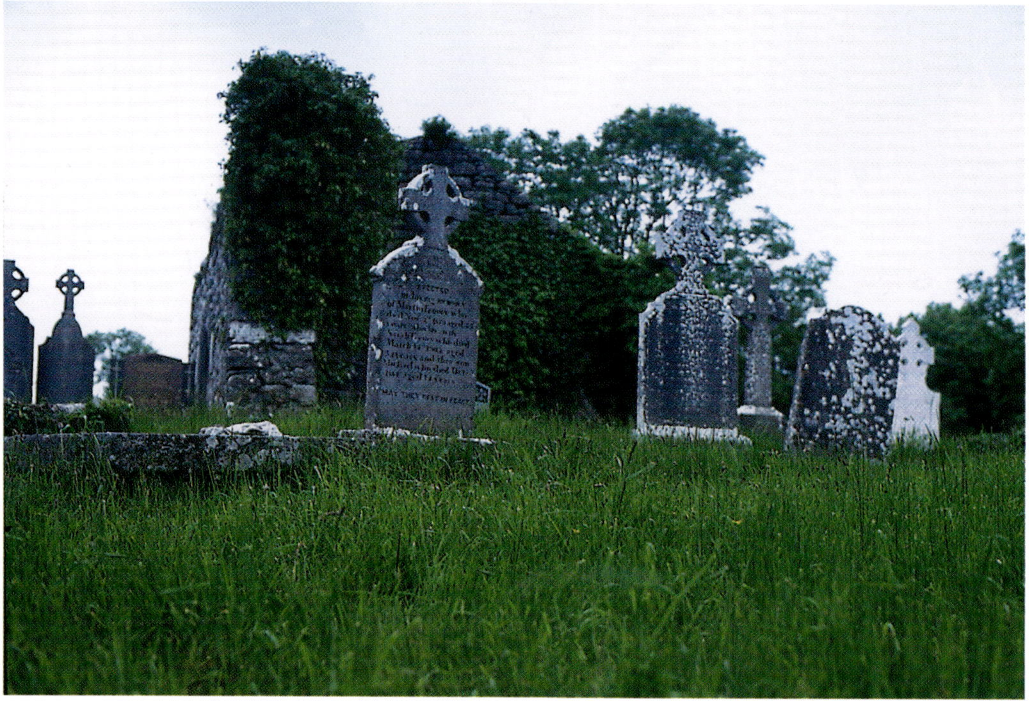

THE POETS CEMETERY, KILLEENEEN, GALWAY.

The poet Raftery was buried here. Anthony Raftery had a marvellous gift for language and his themes ranged from the religious and political debates of the time to love and satire.

OLD THATCH COTTAGE HOUSE, KILLEENEEN, GALWAY.

This restored cottage lies next to the cemetery of the poets.

GALWAY

COOLE LAKE

Yeats was to write in *Dramatis Personae* of the lake;

'In later years I was know the edges of that lake better than any spot on earth, to know it in all the changes of the seasons, to find there is always some new beauty.'

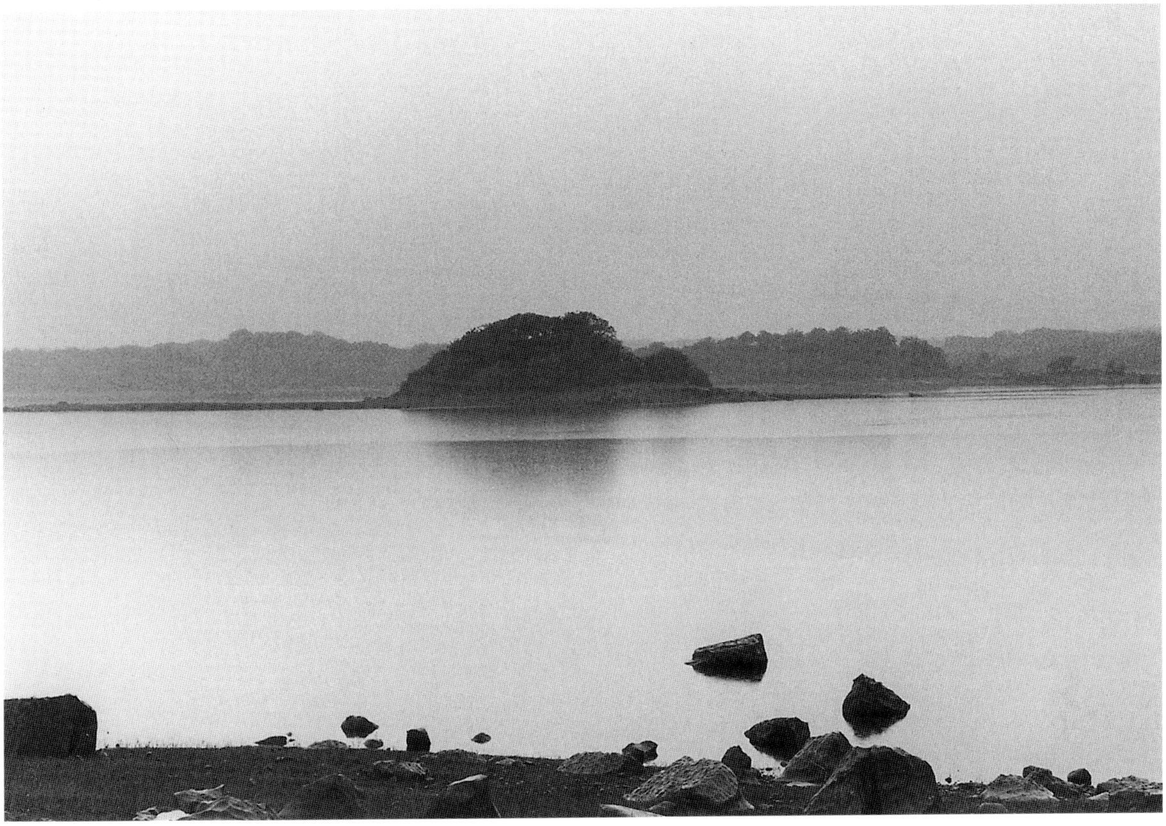

COOLE LAKE

Of the many of strange stories associated with the lake was the following: One person saw two ladies by the shore and at first he thought they were from the house. As he ventured closer, wings appeared upon each and they vanished into thin air.

GALWAY

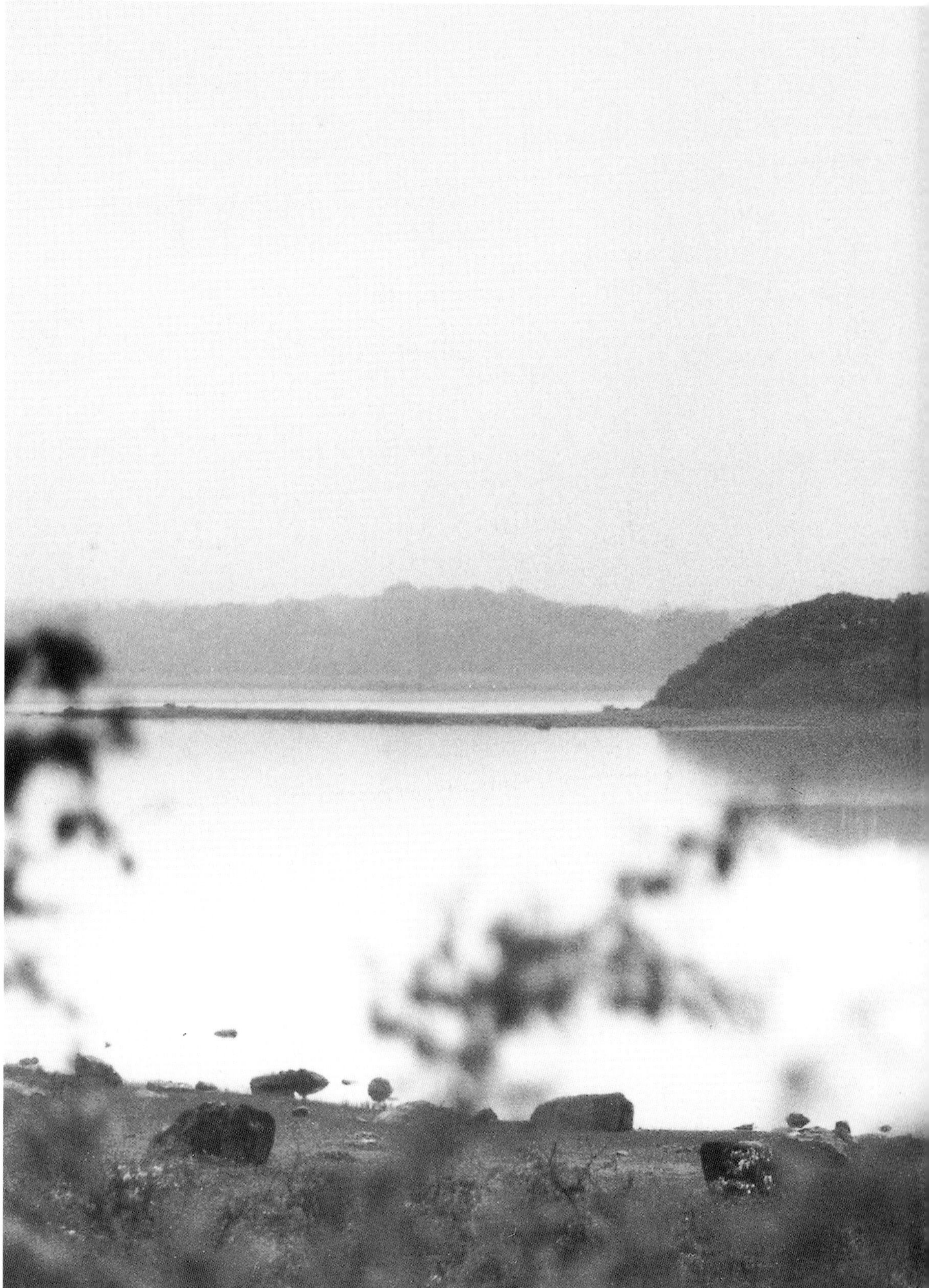

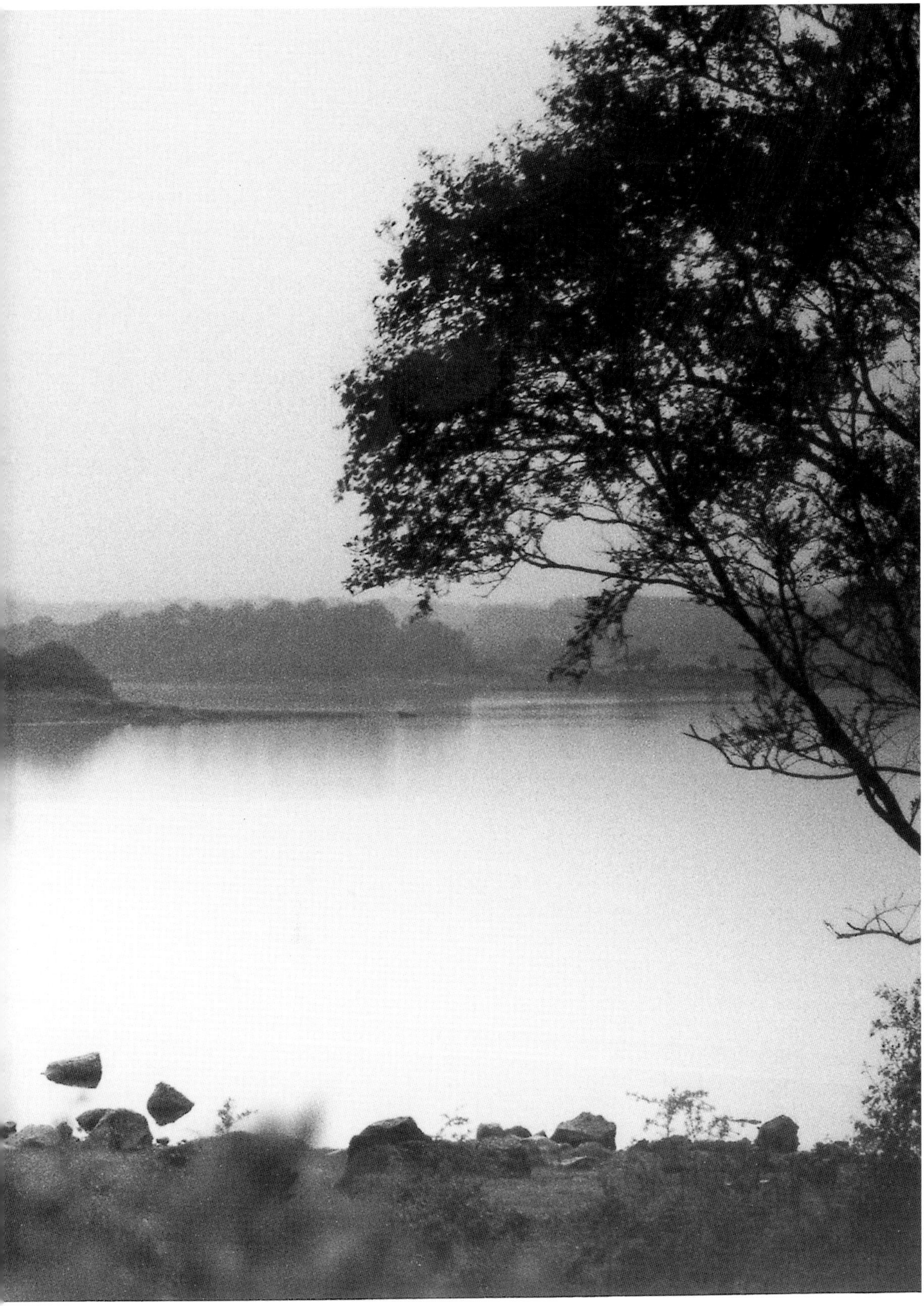

COOLE LAKE

There are many strange happenings associated with the lake and its rivers. The legendary King Guaire on hearing that Saint Colman's mother 'would have a son greater than his', bade his people 'make an end to her before the child is born'. The people then are supposed to have put a heavy stone around her neck and and flung her into the furthest part of the lake, but she didn't sink and came to the shore, eventually giving birth to St Colman.

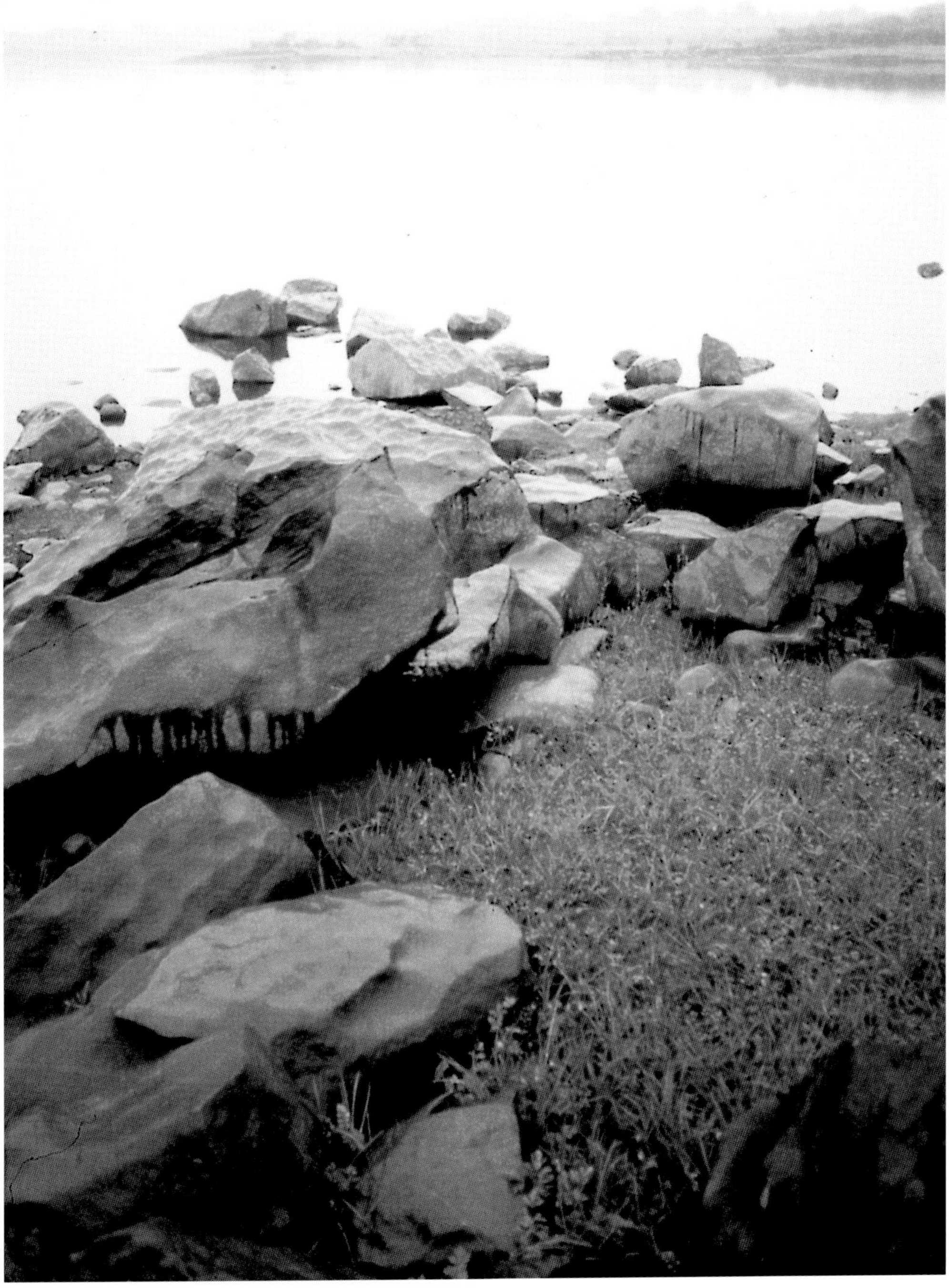

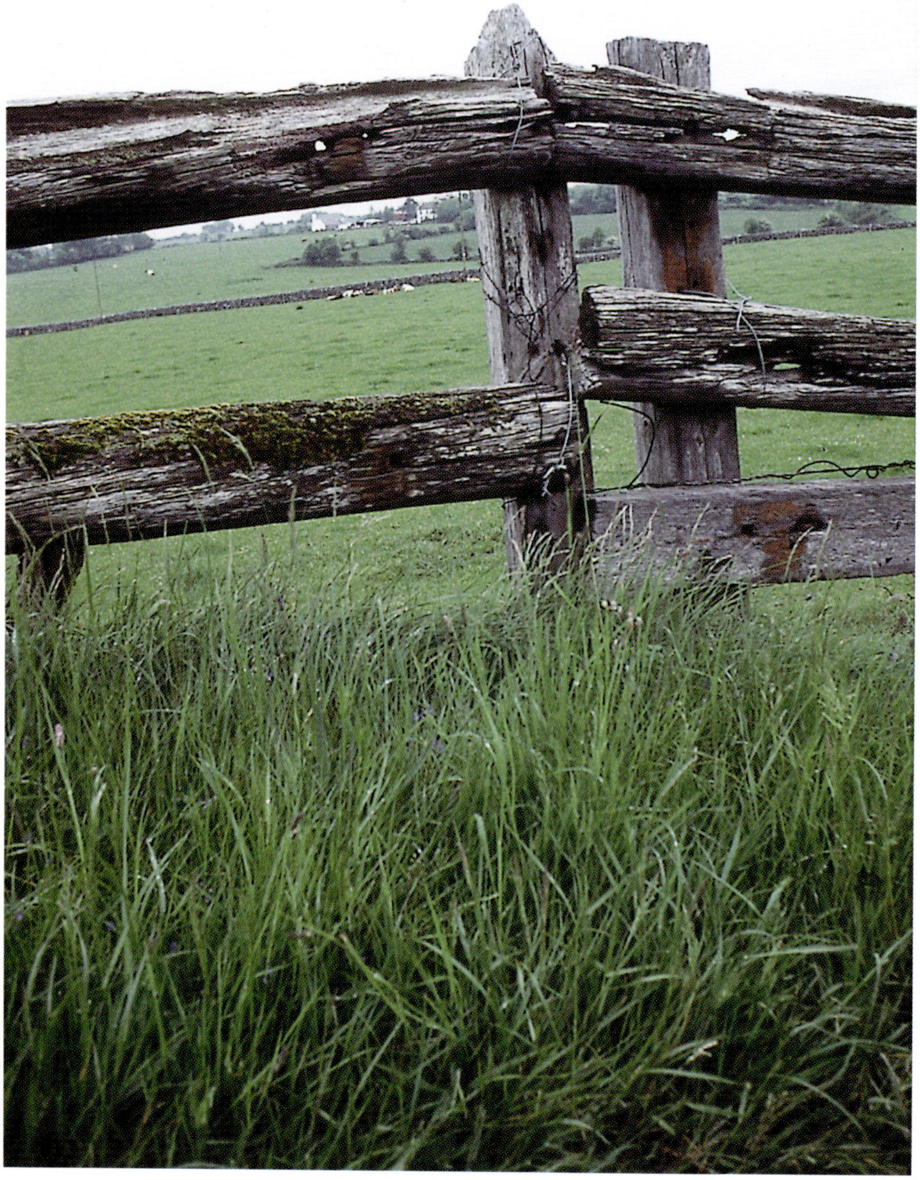

RURAL FENCING IN GALWAY

Many of Galway's quiet country lanes have remained almost unchanged since Yeats day.

COOLE LAKE

Coole park dates from 1768 when a forefather of Lady Gregory's husband bought the estate, then over 600 acres, having made his fortune in the East India Company. Other purchases were made so the estate included over 15,000 acres including Thoor Ballylee, Yeats future home.

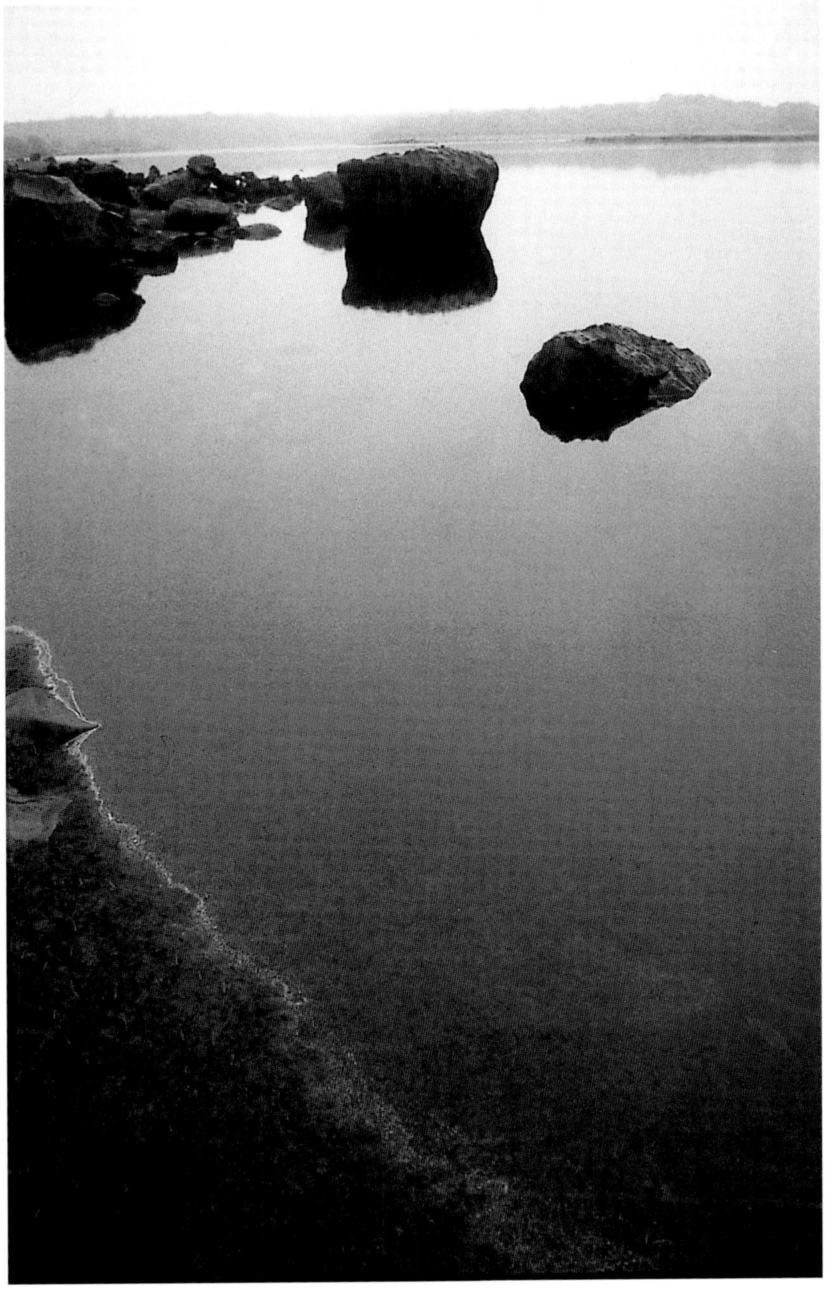